PENGUIN I

NATURAL KINGDOMS

Dr Rajan Sankaran, an internationally renowned homeopath, has been in practice since 1981. He developed the 'sensation method' in homeopathy, on which he gives lectures and seminars throughout the world. Dr Sankaran is the author of several books, including *The Spirit of Homoeopathy*, *The Substance of Homoeopathy*, *The Sensation in Homoeopathy* and *Homoeopathy for Today's World*. He lives in Mumbai and is the head of The Other Song International Academy of Advanced Homoeopathy.

PENGUIN BOOKS
NATURAL KINGDOMS

Dr Rajan Sankaran, an internationally renowned homeopath, has been in practice since 1981. He developed the sensation method of homeopathy, on which he gives lectures and seminars throughout the world. Dr Sankaran is the author of several books, including *The Spirit of Homeopathy*, *The Substance of Homeopathy*, *The Sensation in Homeopathy* and *The Synergy in Homeopathy: Beyond Polarity*. He lives in Mumbai and is the head of The Other Song International Academy of Advanced Homeopathy.

NATURAL
KINGDOMS

HEALING WITH
HOMEOPATHY

DR RAJAN SANKARAN

PENGUIN BOOKS
An imprint of Penguin Random House

PENGUIN BOOKS

USA | Canada | UK | Ireland | Australia
New Zealand | India | South Africa | China

Penguin Books is part of the Penguin Random House group of companies
whose addresses can be found at global.penguinrandomhouse.com

Published by Penguin Random House India Pvt. Ltd
4th Floor, Capital Tower 1, MG Road,
Gurugram 122 002, Haryana, India

Penguin
Random House
India

First published by Penguin Books India 2014

ISBN 9780143422419

For sale in the Indian Subcontinent only

Typeset in Minion Pro by Manipal Digital Systems, Manipal

Printed at Repro India Limited

www.penguin.co.in

MIX
Paper from
responsible sources
FSC® C047271

CONTENTS

Acknowledgements   vii

Prologue: The Postcard   ix

1. Traditional Homeopathy   1

2. Let Dogs Bark   12

3. New Developments in Homeopathy   23

4. The Homeopathic Process   45

5. First Impressions   51

6. Observing the Language of the Patient   68

7. The Problem   79

8. Moment of Crisis   92

9. Dreams and Fears   104

10. Interests and Hobbies   115

11. Relationships   122

12. Childhood   134

Contents

13. Lifestyle   143
14. Advanced Techniques   153
15. Analysis   171
16. What Happened after the Remedy   202
Conclusion   225

Notes   231
Further Reading   239

ACKNOWLEDGEMENTS

Many thanks go to the following persons who helped me with this book:

Armeen Jasavala, Samuel and Lila Flagler, Nishita Shah, Manish Bhatia, Siddharth Dhanvant Shanghvi, Niyati Dhuldhoya, Chinmayee Manjunath and Meghna Shah.

Also, a deep appreciation goes to the three wonderful people who generously permitted me to use their case studies in the book.

Prologue

THE POSTCARD

I did not expect the postcard.

It was a quiet day in January 1979, rather cold for Bombay, as Mumbai was known back then. There was nothing to say. The grief of my father's passing hung heavily in the house. My mother and I had just lost our dearest one to cancer. A six-month agony of hope and pain, and then he left . . . just like that. It was as if the lamp had been blown out and we were in darkness.

Many people came to console me, and I received many letters that told me what a great homeopath my father was, the people he had helped, the students he had taught his craft. But to me, his only child, he could not fully impart his great knowledge. I was just in my first year of homeopathic college. He was gone, his legacy of homeopathy gone with him. How I wished he had stayed a few more years to guide me. How I dreamed of spending some time with him.

Sometimes, I wished I were gone instead of him. But then I decided I had to live up to his name. I had to be the best I could be.

A few days later, I received a postcard. There were very few words on it.

Written in blue ink were the words, 'My condolences at the passing of your father. Let me know if I can be of help.' I had heard these words many times in the last few days, but the signature below these words came as a surprise— S.R. Phatak.

I had met Dr Phatak only once when I had several ulcers on my legs and my father wanted some help in treating me. I remembered the quiet lane in Mumbai in which his house was located. He met patients in a small room in that house. It was an old building where he may have lived for most of his seventy years.

The old doctor had taken one look at me through his thick glasses and asked me a couple of questions about what made the pain better or worse. He seemed to be very interested when I said I could not hang my legs down. Then he looked at my palms and told my father to note that they looked mottled or patchy. He then referred to a small book on his table and suggested a homeopathic remedy.

Dr Phatak was my father's guide in homeopathy. Though my father was considered an authority himself, he would sometimes take unsolved cases to Dr Phatak and seek his advice. Though it was never expressed, the two men had a deep affection for each other. Dr Phatak was a man of few words. Leading an almost ascetic life for the past decade, he was cut off from the world and seldom left his house; my father was both his protégé and colleague.

The postcard expressed no feelings, yet it touched me deeply.

I was now without a father and without a guide. Here was a ray of hope. Homeopathy is a science of treatment based on the idea that disease is not a problem in the parts of the body, the way modern medicine looks at it, but it is a dynamic disturbance of the whole person. Each individual has his own characteristic disturbance, and therefore needs an appropriate, individually chosen remedy. The principles are clear, but the process of identifying the individual remedy for each person by a careful study of his symptoms and personality, and then comparing this with the two thousand or more remedies in homeopathy to find the right one, is an art. Like other art forms, homeopathy is best learned from an accomplished artist.

I answered the letter, thanked him for the postcard and asked him if he would be my guide. His reply came a week later. He asked me to meet him on the Tuesday of the following week at 4 p.m. I was very excited. I was going to meet my father's teacher! Would he find me worthy of learning from him?

I met Dr Phatak on Tuesday, and he was sitting in his room on an easy chair reading an old copy of *Reader's Digest*. He was much older now. He had closed his practice—an old folded stethoscope hung behind him, like a question mark embedded in the wall. His face was expressionless as he looked at me, a boy of nineteen. He seemed tired and reticent. I wondered to myself whether my father's passing had affected him.

After a little while, I asked him if he would be my guide—could I watch him work? He was reluctant and said he had no patients and he had nothing to teach. In fact, he said, it would be better to practise as a skin specialist or a psychiatrist, since they had fewer medicines to choose from and had fewer emergencies. With nothing more to say, he went back to reading the *Reader's Digest*.

He was the most skilled and senior homeopath I knew. He had graduated from a conventional medical college but had become a homeopath fifty years ago. There was so much that I—a novice—could learn from him! An idea suddenly occurred to me. I said, 'Even if you do not teach me, will you help me with some difficult cases, like you did for my father?' Something seemed to stir in him and he agreed.

I had no patients. I was a mere student. I had to find someone to volunteer! My uncle, who suffered from a cough and breathlessness, was an obvious choice. Being a mild and easy man, he let me write down all his symptoms, the way I had learned to in college and from books. The process that homeopaths call 'case taking' involves asking the patient the details of all their symptoms and recording their bodily and mental characteristics.

It takes from one to two hours to go through all the details. Then each aspect of the case is compared with the various remedies known. Indexes of symptoms called repertories aid this process. Dr Phatak had authored a small repertory himself, and it was the one he used most frequently.

I grilled my uncle all I could. I took all the details I could and studied all there was to know about his symptoms. The next Tuesday at 4 p.m. we were at Dr Phatak's door. Dr Phatak carefully read all I had written without uttering a word. I was tense and anxious, just sitting there in anticipation. This was my trial.

Dr Phatak then asked my uncle a couple of questions. They were very sharp, precise questions that elicited the most important characteristics of the case. He had to only glance at those features in his small repertory and then he told me the name of the remedy to be administered. I was crestfallen. My case taking had missed those vital points. I had failed the test. I looked at Dr Phatak's face for any clue. His face was like a sphinx. I took his leave not daring to ask if I could come again. As I was leaving he asked, 'So, next Tuesday?'

It was a great moment in my life. I felt I had been accepted as Dr Phatak's student. My journey as a homeopath had begun.

Each week, I would hunt for people I could take to him as patients. I would ask other homeopaths to let me take some of their patients to him. I even took the cleaning staff of my building to him. Each week, he warmed up to me a bit more. I think more than my ability, he liked my passion and persistence. I watched how he questioned the patients. It was as if he knew where the problem was and with one precise strike, the characteristic of the patient would flow out and the remedy chosen just hit the right spot, and the patient's condition would improve!

I watched how he used his repertory and how he grasped the essence of the remedies. He told me that each remedy represented a personality type. The homeopath should know his patients as if they were close friends. A homeopath should know them so well that he could identify them by the way they walked or even knocked on the door.

Sometimes he would talk a little bit, sometimes he would smile; once in a while he would share an anecdote, like the one about how he started practising homeopathy.

Dr Phatak had started his medical career as a general practitioner and his initiation into homeopathy was a curious one. He once got a patient with a very unusual complaint. The patient said he felt an icy-cold sensation in his upper back, in the area between the scapulae or wing-bones. He had been to several doctors and even the rare neurologist in those times. They had no clue about what to do and had tried several treatments but to no avail.

Dr Phatak had no idea how to treat him either. He gave the patient a vitamin since he had nothing better to try out. That week he was walking on a street that had a second-hand bookshop right on the pavement. Many books lay spread out and a curious Dr Phatak was just glancing at them. His eye fell on a book of homeopathic remedies.

He picked it up. The first few pages were missing and the page that was now the first had a list of symptoms, one of which caught Dr Phatak's attention. It read: 'Sensation of icy coldness between the scapulae.' Dr Phatak had never studied a textbook of modern medicine with this symptom but here it was, in that book—exactly as the patient had described it!

Dr Phatak was intrigued. He read the name of the medicine for the symptom: *Ammonium muriaticum*. This meant nothing to him. He took the book to a homeopathic pharmacy and asked them to give the remedy to him. 'In what potency?' he was asked. He had no idea that homeopathic remedies come in several potencies. He asked the pharmacy person to give him a medium potency, just to try out. He got the 30th potency.

Dr Samuel Hahnemann, who discovered homeopathy two centuries ago, found that through serial dilution and a process of shaking thoroughly, the power of homeopathic remedies increase. Dr Phatak had no idea that the 30th potency he had obtained comprised a dilution comparable to 1 mg of the substance (*Ammonium chloride*) diluted in more water than can be contained in several oceans put together.

The next time the patient came to him and reported no change from the medicines he had been given, Dr Phatak opened the bottle of the tiny sweet homeopathic pills and put three of them on the patient's tongue. He did not expect anything to really happen.

One week later the patient returned. The smile on his face was a telltale sign of what he was about to report. After ten years of having had the complaint, it had vanished within just three days of ingesting the small pills. Dr Phatak's journey as a homeopath had begun. This serendipitous discovery would result in him becoming one of the most skilful homeopaths the world had seen.

As much as I was impressed by his skill in homeopathy, I desired to imbibe something of his spirit as a person. He did not want any approbation and he distanced himself from his achievements.

One year into my time with Dr Phatak, one of my father's friends, Dr Kanjilal from Calcutta (now Kolkata), was visiting Bombay. He was the president of the Homeopathic Medical Association of India and a very well-known homeopath. He became something like a father figure for me after my father's passing. On this visit, he expressed a desire to meet Dr Phatak. I took him with me the following Tuesday.

Dr Phatak peered at him through his thick glasses and asked abruptly, 'What do you want?' Dr Kanjilal, a man with genuine intentions, said, 'Sir, I have come to express my respect and gratitude for all you have done for homeopathy.' Dr Phatak turned to me and spoke in his native language, Marathi, which Dr Kanjilal did not follow. He told me that he would rather not have people come to appreciate his work.

While I listened, the words from the Gita came to my

mind: 'You have the right only to do your duty, not to the fruit therefrom.' Dr Phatak saw himself as the instrument, not as the doer. He felt no attachment to his work.

My Tuesdays with Dr Phatak were the highlight of my life as a student. More and more, I learned to look from his viewpoint at patients and at remedies. The whole world of homeopathy slowly opened up to me. It was as if the masters of the past were alive in Dr Phatak, speaking through his illustrative work. At that time I had no idea that Dr Phatak's book would, in the next two decades, become one of the most widely used books in the profession throughout the world.

Weeks rolled into months, and a few months became two years. Dr Phatak was getting older. He was slowly withdrawing from others even more, or maybe from his own mortal self. Finally, one Tuesday he told me of a case of a child about seven years old. He had come with the complaint of severe constipation and no stools for days. An enema was tried among other things with very temporary relief.

The child was taciturn and he would hardly speak. He would not communicate with his peers. His academic performance had radically dropped. It had all started with the illness of his father who had cancer. A long period of suffering ended in the father's death. The boy had not expressed his grief. A silent witness to these events, the boy had borne it all silently. After his father's demise, the constipation had started.

Dr Phatak looked at me and asked me how I would find a remedy for the child. This came to me as a surprise. He had not asked me such a question before and I felt this was a test. He wanted to see what I had learnt in all those months under his tutelage. I opened the small index of symptoms that Dr Phatak had created: 'Concise Alphabetical Repertory'. Here I searched for the symptom of the child. I looked for remedies under 'Grief', but instinctively felt that there was another way.

Something prompted me to look under 'Constipation' and I read the various subheadings. Then I saw it: 'Constipation from Mental Shock, Nervous Strain'. This is what the boy had undergone: nervous strain from the months of his father's illness and then the shock of his death. The remedy listed for this symptom was *Magnesium carbonicum*. I knew from my limited knowledge that this remedy suits taciturn people, who are not able to express their emotions.

I hesitatingly conveyed my findings to Dr Phatak. A rare smile illuminated his face. He called me close to him and gave me a pat on the back, which I took to be his blessing. Then he said, 'I think I have taught you what I could, I need to rest now.'

At that moment, I knew that my Tuesdays with Dr Phatak were over.

Three decades have passed since. My own journey in homeopathy began with Dr Phatak and then took me to several other masters of that time. My thirst was unquenchable and I plunged myself into both study and practice. I found myself continually amazed by what homeopathy could do. With a group of colleagues I worked to develop the science and art of homeopathy further and finally I came full circle. Dr Phatak's approach, I realized, encapsulated the essence of the practice.

I feel at this point in time I am beginning to get an idea of what homeopathy really is. More importantly, I am beginning to understand what it teaches us about ourselves, our health, our illnesses and our healing.

This book is meant to share just this learning.

1

TRADITIONAL HOMEOPATHY

The Law of Similars

Homeopathic medicine is a medical art based upon fundamental principles that have been effectively used for healing for hundreds of years.

A German physician, Dr Christian Friedrich Samuel Hahnemann (1755–1843), who was totally unhappy with the orthodox medical practice of the eighteenth century, discovered something unique which he called the 'Law of Similars'.

In his attempts to discover why cinchona, the bitter red bark of a tropical tree, was an effective medicine for malaria, he experimented by taking the medicine himself. He developed symptoms of periodic fever and chills, headaches, vertigo, and many symptoms similar to malaria. This led him to postulate that, 'A disease will be cured by a substance that can create a similar state in a person.' This was the birth of the Law of Similars.

This idea can be understood through a very simple example. If a person has recently gone through some tragedy, or the loss of a near one, then his grief is best healed by meeting people in a situation similar to his.

In short, the idea is that a disease can be healed by something that can produce a similar disease. In other words, homeopathy is a system of medicine based on the principle of 'like cures like'.

For example, if a healthy person takes a dose of arsenic not large enough to kill him, he would develop symptoms of vomiting, diarrhoea, cold skin, anxiety, rapid pulse rate and weakness. In smaller doses, when taken over a long time, he would develop a running nose, heavy head, coughing, bronchial catarrh, and later, specific disturbances in the skin and nerves. He will have burning all over—which could be relieved by warmth—frequent thirst for sips of water, fear of death, restlessness and a worsening of symptoms at noon and midnight.

According to the homeopathic law of 'like cures like', countless patients displaying such symptoms have been cured by the homeopathically prepared medicine *Arsenicum album*. This was irrespective of the disease name, be it cholera, colds, eczema, asthma and so on.

Provings

In order to understand what a homeopathic medicine can cure, we must know what symptoms that medicine produces in a healthy human being. 'Provings' are the scientific way in which homeopathic medicines are tested.

In a proving, a homeopathic medicine is administered to healthy volunteers who carefully note down in simple, non-technical language the symptoms that are being experienced and produced after taking the medicine. Both physical and mental symptoms are recorded.

These symptoms are then recorded and arranged, and added to the *Homeopathic Materia Medica*,* an extensive encyclopedia of medicines along with their respective symptoms.

In simpler terms, the *Materia Medica* contains the pure effects of the various homeopathic medicines on healthy persons. The symptoms are very precisely described. These are then systematically recorded and indexed in volumes of books called 'repertories'.

It is not merely written that *Belladonna* produces a headache. It is written that *Belladonna* produces 'aching pain in the right temporal region, which on leaning the head on the hand changes to bursting pain, and extends to the right frontal protuberance'.

---

* See the listings in Further Reading.

This is just one of *Belladonna*'s 1440 symptoms.
There are no simplifications, no presumptions—only exact, meticulous and concrete facts.

One may ask: Why test the medicine on healthy human beings and not on animals?

Simply put, disease has two diverse means of expression. The first is what can be visibly seen, the changes in a person's appearance or in the tissues of their body. These are termed objective symptoms. The second is what is felt. These are termed subjective symptoms, which include types of pain, emotions and other sensations experienced by individuals. These subjective symptoms are enormously significant because they appear before the objective changes and they help individualize a patient in a disease. This is why Dr Hahnemann felt it necessary to test the medicines on healthy human beings.

Dr Hahnemann himself individually tested and recorded the effects of ninety-nine medicines. This has been described as the largest, most accurate and most extensive of investigations into medicinal action made by any single observer throughout the annals of medical history.

Homeopathy uses remedies from the plant, mineral and animal kingdoms and each remedy is tested on healthy volunteers. As mentioned earlier, the symptoms of the body and mind are carefully noted in the *Materia Medica* and indexed in the repertories. When a patient comes for treatment, the symptoms of his body and mind state are carefully noted and then a comparison is made between his symptoms and the symptoms of the various remedies, to find one remedy that most closely matches his symptoms. The remedy is then administered in an ultra-diluted form, known as 'potency'.

Potency

Hahnemann aspired to prove and utilize medicines that were beneficial but known to be fatal or poisonous when ingested in large doses. He discovered a solution to this problem, by reducing the quantity of the drug. As he did this, he found that the destructive or poisonous effects were lessened but, more importantly, the smaller quantity provided a more curative effect.

Progressively, he started bringing down the dose more and more, and started diluting the medicine with a seemingly lifeless medium like water or alcohol. He discovered that when the medicines were so diluted, they not only became completely unharmful, but they acted on the disease even better. He had made another great discovery. In addition to the Law of Similars, he had found immense power in the 'small dose'.

These dilutions are called homeopathic potencies. These potencies are prepared in a very specific and meticulous way.

If the drug is from a liquid, one drop of the drug is

mixed in 99 drops of alcohol. This mixture is given ten jerks or hits (called succussions). This represents the 1st potency of the drug. One drop of the first potency is mixed with another 99 drops of alcohol and given another ten jerks. This represents the 2nd potency of the drug. Subsequent potencies are prepared in a similar manner.

Hahnemann used both soluble and insoluble substances, like gold, copper, silver and mercury, to prepare the solutions. He named the entire process of preparing a homeopathic medicine trituration. By pounding and pulverizing and then mixing with alcohol and water, he produced a solution of these substances.

How these medicines act when diluted to such unbelievable limits still is a confounding mystery that science has not been able to explain for the last two centuries. However, simply through experiments on healthy and sick human beings, it has been observed that potencies act very powerfully.

Through the process of potentization, substances like sand or common table salt, and poisonous substances like arsenic have been converted into powerful healing agents.

When the substance is potentized, and thus refined, then finer and finer qualities of the medicine are revealed. It is not only that a remedy produces broad symptoms like insanity, delirium or mania during testing, but a specific quality of emotions and feelings, which are then recorded diligently in precise detail. When a patient comes with similar symptoms, we choose a remedy matching that exact state of being.

The Force of Life

Hahnemann believed that a force, a vital force of life, which he termed Life Force or Vital Force, governs the human body.

This is the force that coordinates our systems, it has the power to defend us from invading agents, it helps us to fight back when we are sick, repairs our damaged tissues, and makes us grow and develop.

The body is subjected to a number of assaults at every moment and at every turn. Changes in the weather, changes in the strains of disease, physical and mental trauma, are just a few of them. In all instances we come in contact with innumerable germs. They are everywhere: in the air we breathe, in the pores of our skin and in every fold of our body.

This Life Force within each one of us organizes our system and helps preserve the equilibrium between us and our surroundings. It is our resistance power, our immunity, and our way to combat these assaults.

Homeopathic medicines aim to restore the overall health of the patient—by treating the cause—not just eliminate the symptoms. When the patient becomes healthy, the symptoms disappear.

A migraine or dermatitis is not the disease—it is the end product of the disease. The real sickness is in the disturbance of the normal functioning of the vitality, the Vital Force. Homeopathic drugs correct this disturbance through treating the root cause.

How the Medicine Works

To understand how homeopathic medicine works, let us take an example. Imagine a patient who suffers from migraines. What we need to understand is that 'migraine' is just a name, or, in homeopathic terms, a local manifestation of a certain systemic problem. Basically, migraines are an affection of the nerves. In these patients, nervous sensitivities are very high and there are various triggering factors like stress, emotive factors, sunlight, motion, noise, etc. As a result of the nerves being oversensitive to certain triggers, they produce pain and headache. The oversensitive nature of the nerves is not an isolated phenomenon. It can be a part of the axis that controls the body, comprising namely the endocrine system (hormones), immunological system and the mind. These three form an axis that acts as a regulator of the body.

Disease exists only if there is a central disturbance of the axis. We have to identify what the central disturbance is in this person. How do the nervous system, endocrine system, immune system and the mind of the individual work? This gives us a picture of the central disturbance within the patient, and when that is accurately found and the appropriate remedy matched, the local expressions automatically disappear, because they are merely expressions of the central disturbance.

Holism and Individualism

Fundamental to homeopathic philosophy is the tenet that disease is not an affection of the separate parts of the body but of a person as a whole, and that each person has his own individual disease or state, and the changes in the organs are only the result of this state.

The idea of *holism* suggests that the body is born as one, functions as one, reacts as one and dies as one. When affected by sickness, it reacts as a whole. The symptoms represent this very reaction and are found all over the body, and also in the patient's mental state.

If we want to get a true and complete picture of the sickness, we must not only consider the chief complaint of the patient, but also the symptoms manifested in all parts of the body and mind. Homeopaths give a single medicine in order to heal the patient as a whole and to remove his ailments.

Homeopathy not only recognizes that the mind and body are two parts of a whole, but also that they are closely tied together.

A good homeopath learns to perceive disease as a continually evolving process, which begins in the womb and ends in the tomb. The homeopath will go into great details of each symptom at all stages in the patient's development, physically and mentally, in an effort to find out what differentiates one patient from another.

The concept of *individualization* is very important in homeopathic medicine. No two people are alike. Similarly, no two people react alike in sickness, even if they suffer from the same complaint.

The patient's language and speech, doodles, hand gestures, handwriting, manner of dressing, choice of profession, and the way he presents his complaints, all of these individualize him. Each of these above-mentioned aspects will be explained in further detail throughout the book.

Homeopathy is essentially the treatment of the individual patient. The homeopath considers, studies and treats the patient individually.

A father and daughter once came to my clinic, both with a diagnosis of cervical spondylosis. The father's pain worsened in winter and in the morning. He had constipation alternating with diarrhoea. His appetite was variable and he liked sweets. He felt no thirst, and experienced sleeplessness. Mentally, he was anxious, mild, preferred company, and wept easily. Conversely, the daughter's pain was worse in summer and in the sun. Her appetite was lower than normal and she hated sweets. She was extremely irritable and preferred to remain alone.

Although the label of the disease was the same, the

picture was vastly different. In fact, they each suffered from their own peculiar disease. Therefore, each one required a different medicine. Homeopathic medicine is prescribed on the basis of an individual patient's troubles and not for the name of the disease he has. Thus, ten patients of asthma may require ten different medicines.

It is the inner disturbance or upsetting of the Vital Force that needs to be corrected and restored to a healthy balance. In homeopathy, disease is seen as an affection of the whole person, and so the treatment is holistic as well as individualistic. As Dr Hahnemann, the father of homeopathy, once said:

> Now, as certainly as we should listen particularly to the patient's description of his sufferings and sensations, and attach credence especially to his own expressions wherewith he endeavours to make us understand his ailments . . . so certainly, on the other hand, in all diseases . . . the investigation of the true, complete picture and its peculiarities demands especial circumspection, tact, knowledge of human nature, caution in conducting the inquiry and patience in an eminent degree.[1]

2

LET DOGS BARK

The man who sat facing me was exactly twice my age. I was forty years old and he was eighty. There was a big table between us and on it was a copy of the latest issue of an international journal of homeopathy. It was January 2000. We were in my office on the second floor of a building in a busy Mumbai street. One could hear the noises of the street—buses, cars and the incessant honking. We were accustomed to these noises. However, on that day it felt strangely quiet. It felt as though only he, I and the journal existed.

~

I had met Roheetbhai fifteen years earlier, in 1985. I was then in the early years of my homeopathic practice in Mumbai, and I also used to sit in once a week with a senior homeopath, Dr Sarabhai.

During that time, Dr Sarabhai was asked to speak at a homeopathic conference and had asked me to come along. I was then very interested in diabetes and had read up quite a bit on the subject. The so-called complications of diabetes, which had so far been attributed to high blood sugar, occurred due to changes in the small blood vessels. A researcher named Marvin Siperstein found in 1970 that the blood vessel changes precede the increase in blood sugar, leading to the question 'What is diabetes?' After Dr Sarabhai spoke at the conference, he suggested that I add a few comments. I took the opportunity and shared with the audience whatever I had read up on the subject.

Among those who had come to the conference was a very young homeopathy graduate, Kshitij, who conveyed the summary of the proceedings to his father, Roheetbhai.

Roheetbhai was at that time a very senior homeopath with a huge practice fairly close to my clinic. It was a big surprise to receive a phone call from him the day after the event. He introduced himself and asked if I could go and visit a patient of his who had been admitted to a nearby nursing home with a non-healing ulcer on his thigh, a complication of his long-standing diabetic condition. I wondered why such a senior homeopath was asking me, a fledgling, to advise on such a complicated case.

I was at the nursing home the next day. The patient was about fifty years old and had a huge ulcer on his thigh; the flesh had been eaten up until his bone. Despite many different treatments, it had shown no sign of healing. I did what I had learnt in homeopathy. I started noting his case details.

When I had completed the process, Roheetbhai walked into the room. This was the first time we were meeting each other. He gently asked me what my conclusion was. I shared with him my analysis and opined that the remedy that could help was *Phosphorus*. I suggested that the patient be given only one dose and we could wait and see its effects. Roheetbhai gave me an incredulous look but was willing to go along for the time being.

I kept in touch with Roheetbhai's patient every day. On the third day he showed some signs of change. He felt better on the whole, which is a very important factor for the homeopath because homeopathy holds that disease affects the whole person, and the cure starts with a sense of general well-being. By the end of the week, the ulcer showed signs of healing and by the second week the change was significant.

Roheetbhai called me again that week. He wanted me to see another patient in my office. This was a journalist with tubercular lymph glands who reacted badly to modern antibiotics and wished to take homeopathic medicine. We set up an appointment for 8 a.m. on the coming Wednesday.

Promptly at 8 a.m. the next Wednesday the patient walked into my office and, to my surprise, Roheetbhai accompanied her. He sat by patiently as I took her case details. She was thirty-two, unmarried, very insecure, and liked to eat eggs and chocolate. She perspired profusely from her scalp at night.

Roheetbhai made a note of these symptoms in a small diary that he had brought with him. When I suggested that the patient be treated with the homeopathic remedy *Calcarea carbonica* (an extremely diluted form of calcium carbonate), he nodded in agreement and the two of them left my office.

Two weeks later he called with good news: the patient was feeling much better and her tubercular glands had reduced significantly. He also had a request for me: could he bring one difficult patient to me from his practice every Wednesday at 8 a.m.? I happily agreed.

Each week he would come with one or two patients. We would sit together while I took the case history, studied the repertories and chose the remedy. Roheetbhai would take some notes in his diary and then leave with the patient and continue to treat them on the lines I had suggested. This routine went on uninterrupted for the next twenty-five years until Roheetbhai passed away in 2010.

I met some of these patients after his passing, and they told me that Roheetbhai would say that he wanted to consult with another homeopath for their case. Given that Roheetbhai was quite old, they would expect him to take them to someone more senior than him. When Roheetbhai brought them to me, a homeopath who was less than half his age, they took some time to get over the shock. Roheetbhai was not bothered by this. He was very confident of what he did and was assured of his patients' faith in him. They revered him, and for good reason. He would do anything for them and took great personal care. He was their doctor, adviser, mediator, guide, sympathizer and friend. His word was gospel.

Roheetbhai came to my office to seek my advice on some cases and to understand my training in homeopathy. The knowledge of the repertories and my one-pointed focus stood me in good stead as many cases improved. However, I soon realized that while I had one good quality, Roheetbhai had all the others. His mere presence brought peace to the room. He had a lot of space for others, and the ability to listen and care. These were healing qualities. He epitomized the words of Tinsley Harrison who edited the *Principles of Internal Medicine*: 'The real secret in the care of the patient is caring for the patient.'

I started looking forward to Wednesdays and spending time with Roheetbhai. My technical skill coupled with his human understanding formed a synergy of the head and heart that was palpable in the room.

There were moments between the visits of two patients when we would talk. I would tell him about the challenges I faced, the music I loved, about spirituality and about life. He would listen with keen interest, with a smile on his face that indicated that he had been there and done that. Sometimes, he would share aspects of his life with me. I became his confidant. A close bond formed between us. I would introduce him to my friends, and they all grew very fond of him. He would delight in telling them the story of his own healing.

He recalled that he had developed angina pectoris, which signalled a blockage in the heart vessels. He had approached me and asked for medicine. He remembered that I had told him I would treat him under two conditions. Without asking what they were he had said immediately, 'I agree to your conditions. Now tell me what they are.'

One condition was that I would not reveal the name of the remedy. The second condition was that he would not self-medicate while he was under my treatment. Years after he had recovered, he would humorously narrate that he had recognized his own case report from a book I had written and learnt that the remedy given to him was *Aurum metallicum*, or gold.

~

As the years rolled by, my passion for homeopathy led me to a relentless search for a method that would make both the choice of the remedy and the results in practice more certain. Traditionally, homeopathy relies solely on symptoms. The numerous symptoms of the patient are matched with the symptoms of the 2000 or so remedies to find one among them that best suit the patient.

While this is very effective in some cases, it fails in others because of the heavy reliance on symptoms. If you take one set of symptoms, it points to one remedy, while in the same patient if we choose even a slightly different set of symptoms, it leads to an entirely different remedy. So while homeopaths have often produced brilliant cures, the consistency of their results has not been uniform.

A few colleagues and I worked night and day to find a solution to this problem. Through our research, it became clear to me that each individual person has a specific state of mind that comes from the way he perceives reality. On looking deeper into each individual, we can see that there are three distinct patterns of perception.

One way of looking at reality is that the person feels that he lacks something in himself or has something that he is about to lose. Another perspective is that there is a change in the patient's external reality, which he needs to adapt to. The third way of perceiving is that the world is a fight for survival, and one has to fight or compete.

To take an example, if faced with a sudden business setback, one person can look at it as a loss in one's financial structure and feel the need to do something to restore it. Another person can experience it as a shock and react with panic. The third can see it as a fight with his competitor. Each individual will have one specific type of response to nearly all the events in his life. It is as if each one is programmed to perceive and react in that specific way to all situations.

Homeopathic remedies are drawn from mineral, plant and animal sources and embody the spirit of their source. Through my experience I have found that people who did well on remedies from the mineral kingdom had issues with lacking or losing structure, people who needed remedies from the plant kingdom had issues of sensitivity and reactivity due to a change in circumstances, and people who did well on animal remedies had issues of competition and survival as their core experience of life.

This discovery paved the way for another route of finding the homeopathic remedy for patients, besides the traditional one of using symptoms exclusively.

Now we could not only match the symptoms to the precise remedy but also confirm that the remedy was from the kingdom that matched the deepest experience of the patient. This discovery led the way for a further sub-classification within the kingdoms, so that we could know not only the kingdom the patient belonged to but also identify which precise group or class within that kingdom the patient was closest to. For example, we could say that a patient had features of the reptile class in the animal kingdom or of the lily family in the plant kingdom.

The identification of the features of each subclass was the result of a detailed and painstaking study, which culminated in the publication of several books on the subject. These new ideas on homeopathy not only helped my practice tremendously, but also became very popular among a large section of the homeopathic community. However, some traditional homeopaths were strongly critical of this approach.

~

My ideas and books were being reviewed in homeopathy journals across the world. The journal that lay on the table between Roheetbhai and me was the latest issue of one of the leading journals of homeopathy in the world. For this millennium issue, the editors had decided to interview some of the most well-known homeopaths across the globe about their views on where homeopathy was and where it was going.

The silence in the room was palpable because the interviews had come as a shock. On page after page, I had been criticized and accused by well-known traditional homeopaths who did not agree with my ideas. My ideas were also grossly misunderstood and misrepresented. One homeopath even said: 'Sankaran alone has done more harm to homeopathy than all the enemies of homeopathy together.'

When I first read these interviews, I got very agitated. Many thoughts crossed my mind. I felt panicky. Was this the end of my career? I experienced strong self-doubt. Was I guilty of harming my precious homeopathy so grievously? I also felt anger, and perhaps even some malice, towards these colleagues who I felt were maligning me. The editors had asked me to write a response.

My agitation did not subside quickly, and I waited to

share these developments with Roheetbhai. When he walked into my clinic, he immediately sensed something was amiss. I briefly told him what had happened. We saw a couple of patients and after we'd finished we sat some moments in silence with the journal between us.

Roheetbhai didn't say much. He looked at me intensely with those sharp eyes of his, and then, very unexpectedly, he broke into song. In a sonorous voice he sang the lines of the sixteenth-century Indian saint Kabir. The words can be roughly translated as: 'Let your mind be attuned to the higher truth while the world engages in petty quarrels. Just as the elephant walks at its own pace, not bothered about the dogs that bark at it.'

When he finished singing these lines he came over to me, gently touched my back and left. I realized he had just conveyed to me the very essence of his life in that song. One had to do what one felt was right, unconcerned with what others felt or commented. I re-examined all the work I had done up until then, and felt convinced that it was the way to go ahead and that I was doing the right thing. I needed to work more along those lines and try to perfect the system I had initiated.

That night I was clear about my response to the journal. There was no more self-doubt. I wrote,

I have chosen to not react to the many personal comments about me. . . . I invite my critics to Bombay, where it will be my pleasure to show them case videos and actual patients.

21

I will show them cases in which I arrived at a remedy using these new ideas and where traditional methods failed in bringing the solution. If they can show me how one can solve these cases without any of these newer ideas, I am willing to learn. And if this is not possible and they feel that my ideas indeed have some scope, then they can study them and apply them, and then offer more constructive criticism, which will be welcome from such learned and experienced persons.

More than ten years later, my ideas became so widespread that when I did an online lecture series, it was attended by homeopathic practitioners from forty-three nations. Spread over eighteen months, this was called 'Wednesdays with Rajan', with gratitude to Roheetbhai, to whom I dedicated the course.

It took several more years to understand the deeper meaning of Kabir's song. The dogs that bark are not outside, but within our own mind. The unaffected elephant symbolizes the witness within us that can keep distance from all the noise in our mind and keep our awareness in the silent, timeless, formless, nameless presence that exists within us.

3

NEW DEVELOPMENTS
IN HOMEOPATHY

After thirty-three years of practising homeopathy and having seen thousands of patients, I can say that our individual perception and reaction to situations is at the root of our stress, and at the root of the 'dis-ease' within us. Stress does not originate from the outside world. It originates from how we experience and how we respond to our outer reality. When we can understand that inner experience, we see a pattern. It is a pattern of inner sensations. The pattern can be classified into three major types.

Let's start with a simple example.

When a patient comes to me for a problem like depression, migraine, asthma, ulcerative colitis or any other physical complaint, I ask them what triggered this physical complaint, or what was the stressful situation in their life to cause this, they say, 'I have disappointment in love'.

From here, we must try to understand the stress-inducing factor: disappointment in love. We need to understand how the patient *as an individual* perceived this. At an emotional level, most people will tell you 'I feel sad, I feel upset, I feel betrayed' and so on. A homeopath would then ask, 'What is your experience of this disappointment?' We see that at an experiential level, there are three patterns.

One girl may tell you, 'I feel shocked! How could this happen? He was talking to me so nicely until yesterday and today he is off! I am shocked! I feel numb.'

The second girl may tell you, 'I was so dependent on this person, he was everything to me. He made all my decisions for me, supported me. He was my friend, and now without him how will I live?'

Then there is a third pattern with the girl saying, 'I think he has gone off with another woman. First, I will destroy her and then I will destroy him!'

These are the three distinct patterns that I have observed in the deepest experience of individuals. Through extensive research, I have found that these relate to the three kingdoms of nature, that is, plant, mineral and animal kingdoms.

Plants have to do with sensitivity and reactivity. In human beings, the plant experience is that of sensitivity. They are affected by many things and must adapt and adjust to them. Minerals have to do with structure. In a mineral personality, we see that they are very systematic and tend to be highly organized. Problems occur when there is a break in structure or organization, relationships or performance. In experiences of the animal kingdom, there are issues of survival and competition, and a play of victim and aggressor, sexuality and attractiveness.

We all have one of these patterns inside us, dominant at a certain time. That's what makes each one of us perceive and react to stress in a specific way.

This is the *other song* playing within you. There is a human song—you as a human being, as an individual and as a part of society. Then, inside you, there is an animal song, a mineral song or a plant song. Your perception of and reaction to reality will be determined by which other song is playing within you at that time. It will determine what you do, how you think and how you feel. It will affect how you talk, how you walk, how you work and your recreational interests.

Stress is not from the outside, but from your experience of what's outside. Your experience is an internal pattern. That pattern mirrors a plant, animal or mineral. With the appropriate homeopathic remedy, from the appropriate kingdom and sub-kingdom that matches your symptom, the internal pattern diminishes. You then react to reality as it is, not from your pattern. You experience the freedom 'to be present in the moment'. When you're free, you become an instrument of the Universe that acts through you.

That is health.

As a homeopathic practitioner, I sit with the patients and try to understand their deepest experiences in several different situations. As I listen, I am able to trace a common pattern which is the connecting thread in all of the patient's stories or experiences. This in homeopathic terms is called the 'Sensation'. Once the *sensation*, or golden thread, has been found and understood, then one can approach the search for the medicine in two ways.

The first way is through comparing the patient's symptoms to the symptoms of the various remedies in homeopathy and finding a pattern that matches with one of them. This is the more traditional way to approach a homeopathic case. The other way that the identified pattern—the sensation—of patients can be analysed is through a novel development in homeopathy, the idea of the natural kingdoms.

Central to the homeopathic approach is understanding, knowing and treating the patient as an individual, instead of treating his symptoms alone. During the case taking, the homeopath goes with the patient through a process of self-discovery. The ultimate goal is to identify the core pattern in each individual that underlies all aspects of his being. This core pattern is the cause of the individual's suffering. The discovery of this pattern helps the practitioner identify the homeopathic remedy for that person. The process helps the patient himself to become more aware of what lies within him, how he perceives and reacts to the world. This awareness is hugely beneficial to both the practitioner and the patient. Through homeopathy I got certain insights into the nature of human beings that are universally applicable.

Whether you believe in homeopathy or not, these insights will help everyone see what lies deeper, at the core of their thoughts, feelings, expressions, behaviour, relationships, dreams, and all aspects of life. What is interesting about this process of examining various aspects and going deeper into them is that it is not interpretative. That means we do not interpret any expression of the individual like his dreams, behaviour, and so on. The process is one of fine observation of all aspects of an individual's being that allows you to see the commonalities at a deeper level. The idea is that all expressions of an individual come from a core experience or sensation, the individual's particular way of perceiving the world.

This sensation is also experienced physically, as physical symptoms and pathology. In order to understand patients at the deepest of levels and prescribe the best homeopathic medicine, the following questions are vital for the homeopath to consider:

— What is it that makes us individuals?
— What is it that makes us perceive and react to reality in our unique way?
— What is it that underlies our various experiences?

All of us feel emotions, such as anger, grief, fear, anxiety and joy, yet each of us feels a different kind of anger, a different degree of grief, a different reason for joy or anxiety, and have a different thing to fear. The difference in the emotions depends upon what we are sensitive to, which in turn depends upon how we perceive reality.

The Three Kingdoms and the Other Song

Through extensive and rigorous research I have discovered that there is a distinct pattern in each kingdom:

— The Plant Kingdom has a pattern of Sensitivity and Reactivity
— The Mineral Kingdom has a pattern of Structure and Function
— The Animal Kingdom has a pattern of Competition and Survival

Each individual has his life as a human being, singing his own human song. However, upon looking deeply, we find that simultaneously, in each person, there is also a whole different story, a whole *other song*, from another non-human world that seems to sing a whole different tune altogether.

At any given time, the deepest level of experience in our pattern, or our other song, falls usually in one of these three kingdoms of nature. Let us take a simple example. An employee has done something wrong and, as a result, his boss yells at him. He can react in one of three ways:

a. He is mortified, feels indignant, and trembles with anger. He is very sensitive and touchy. This is the Plant experience.

b. He feels very insecure, as though he may lose his job. Therefore, his financial security will be affected. He is anticipating a loss of structure, of something he has. This is the Mineral experience.

c. He feels victimized. His boss is more powerful than

him and is able to persecute and victimize him in this manner. He is now thinking of ways to get back at his boss. This is the Animal experience.

Of course, there will be many types of experiences, but generally, most experiences will fall into one of these three main categories. The plant, mineral and animal kingdoms are very broad categories. Each kingdom has been further divided into sub-kingdoms, families and classes, each with its own specific quality and pattern. There is further differentiation in terms of which kind of animal pattern, plant family pattern or mineral pattern one has. For example, a patient can have the pattern of a mammal, bird or a reptile in the animal kingdom. Next, if a patient belongs to the plant kingdom he can have a pattern that resembles the sunflower, cactus or magnolia family, etc. If a person falls in the mineral kingdom, he could have a pattern of silver or gold or any of the hundreds of minerals, salts and compounds.

These patterns have been clearly studied and differentiated in homeopathy. What we observe is that when this pattern is seen in a person, it is to be found not only in one area, but in every area of his life.

Suppose we go back to the previous example of disappointment in love. One person experiences it as shock, another experiences it as a loss of something she needs, and the last one experiences it as having become the victim of a rivalry. In every area of life, the person's experience will lead in the same direction. For example, if we were to ask

29

these three people about their interests and hobbies, the mineral person would say she likes to collect things, put things in order or make structures. The plant person would say she likes to be out in nature, she likes colours and she is sensitive to all of these things. The animal person may say that she likes to be in a competitive sport or activity. Again, when we look at the dreams of these individuals, we see the same experience. The dream of the mineral person may be the death or loss of a relative. The dream of a plant person may be a fearful or scary situation to which they react with fright. The animal person may have somebody coming and hitting or strangulating them, and them trying to overpower him. It is a trial of strength, and who is stronger or weaker.

In this way, in whichever area we observe the patient we see the same pattern. This fixed pattern is to be healed. Patients will experience the same sensation across their mental, emotional and physical states, which makes them unique and individual.

For example, a young man around twenty-five years old came to me with some psychiatric problems. He had insomnia, he used to be extremely restless, and his mental development was not congruent with his age. At times, he was even violent.

He was tall and physically well developed. When I asked him about his nature and about himself, he spoke in a very excited manner. I also observed he spoke in a very childish way. He said, 'In my childhood, I was not good at studies and would spend three to four years in each grade. I was usually the tallest guy in the class and also the most backward in studies. Other classmates would tease me. Sometimes they would get up and stand on a bench, flick my ear and run away. I would get very annoyed with them so I thought I would teach them a lesson. So what I did when there was an examination, I went to the teachers' room, copied all the questions of the test paper and distributed it to all the children in my class. They all got excellent marks. Then, when it was time for the final examination, I wrote down some questions and told them this was the final examination paper. They all believed me, so they did not study, and they all failed. It was just something I had made up, not the final paper at all! That is how I got my revenge on them.'*

After he described his symptoms, I decided to treat him with a remedy called *Bufo rana*.[1] The main symptoms of a person who needs this remedy are a childish mentality, accompanied by physical growth, and revengeful and deceitful tendencies. With this remedy the patient's overall state improved.

Another time, a Catholic priest came to me with Lyme disease, which is a bacterial infection caused by a tick bite, causing problems in the joints, heart and nervous system. He taught neurolinguistic programming and travelled all over the world.

His symptoms were of stiffness and tightness in the

---

* The language the patients have used has been largely left untouched, except to facilitate clarity.

back, with difficulty with first movement. However, with continued movement, the stiffness eased up. What was interesting was his desire to be in constant motion. He moved from one place to another and he was also very physically active. At the age of seventy-five, he still played basketball!

His state of mind from what I understood of him was unique. He said that he would get anxious before going for a basketball game, lecture or presentation. I asked him what the experience of the anxiety was. He said, 'The experience was of tightness. My whole body would become stiff. My stomach muscles would feel tight and stiff. As I would play or speak, the stiffness improved.'

As we can see, this patient's common experience in the physical and mental complaint was of sensitivity and he reacted to the situation with a specific sensation of tightness and stiffness. The way he described his anxiety is exactly how he explained the complaint of his joints.

He got the remedy *Rhus tox*,[2] which is from the plant kingdom. Each medicine from this plant family when proved by healthy humans had the common sensation of stiffness and tightness. With this remedy, the priest's Lyme disease went away. His anxiety and pre-performance stress also disappeared.

And this was how I learned to bring a mental or emotional experience to a Sensation experience. I was able to see the connection between his body and mind so beautifully!

Thirteen years ago, I also dealt with the case of a man with orbital haemangioma. Orbital haemangioma is a blood-vessel tumour situated just behind the eyeball and is extremely dangerous. If the blood vessel ruptures, there can be a serious problem. He was advised to have surgery that would have to cut through his skull and his brain to find the tumour and remove it.

When I met him, I asked him, 'Tell me, what is the experience of the tumour for you?'

His experience was one where his eyes were not coordinated with each other, because one of his eyes was bulging. I asked, 'What is the importance of this coordination for you?'

He said, 'Coordination is the most important thing.' Because he was a performer, his entire ability to perform as a big executive depended on coordination. So everything had to be perfectly coordinated for him. He said, 'First, I would never have my socks not coordinated with my tie.' Even his underwear had to be perfectly coordinated! I asked him to tell me more about this. He said, 'It is true in every area of my life. My hobby is to fly and what is flying for me? It is control and performance and coordination. What is my work for me? It's presentation and coordination.'

He needed a remedy from the mineral kingdom, because his experience was one of needing capability and control in his performance. He was given the remedy *Argentum nitricum*, or silver nitrate in an ultra-diluted dose.

After two months of treatment, his MRI report showed

that the blood-vessel tumour was almost non-existent. There was a 90 per cent major reduction in its size.

Travelling to the Deeper Experiences of an Individual

Reshma, a young woman of thirty-three years, had been under my treatment for a couple of years for multiple sclerosis (MS). The diagnosis of MS itself doesn't indicate what remedy a patient needs. MS is an autoimmune disorder. This means that instead of fighting outside agents such as bacteria or a virus, the immune system is fighting its own healthy cells.

MS also means that the immune system is functioning in a very unhealthy manner and unless this is corrected, there will be no long-term solution to this disease. Corticosteroids and other immunity modulators are used as treatment, but usually have only short-term effects because the basic problem remains uncorrected. The immune system, which is malfunctioning is also not an isolated entity—it is part of the psycho-neuro-endocrine-immune system axis (PNEI).

The mind, the nerves, the hormones and the immune system all function in association with each other. It, therefore, became important to study Reshma's mind, her nervous sensitivity, her hormonal functioning and, finally, all the symptoms she had.

In the initial stages of treatment, I asked Reshma to describe herself as an individual. She said that she worried about very small things and that she was a perfectionist.

Her marriage had ended in a divorce, although she had tried to save it. She had dreamt of having a happy family, but had somehow faced rejection, and often felt unloved and rejected. When rejected she felt numb and confused.

When younger, she would have convulsions when her teachers reprimanded her. Often she held her emotions within herself and did not express them to anyone. Reshma had a history of facial paralysis and blurry vision in the right eye. These two symptoms were the result of MS. Emotionally, she felt a lot of anxiety and grief, a sense of rejection, disappointment and shock.

When she first came to me, I attempted to find a remedy that matched her mental make-up. *Ignatia* is one such remedy that has feelings of unshared grief, disappointment, rejection, shock and being benumbed. I gave Reshma this remedy, only to get a partial response. Reshma kept following up regularly with me every two months and I kept looking for an opening that would take us to a deeper level of her experience.

Through research and experience in several cases, I discovered that each of us can experience reality at one of seven levels:

Level 1: Name
Level 2: Fact
Level 3: Emotions/Feeling
Level 4: Delusions/Imagination
Level 5: Sensation/Experience
Level 6: Energy
Level 7: Witnessing

In the case-taking process, the most superficial level is the name of the disease and diagnosis. For example, rheumatoid arthritis, diabetes, eczema or the flu. In this case, MS is the diagnosis. A homeopath is unable to do much with this information because the name of the disease tells him little about the person's core individual experience. Therefore, the homeopath needs to find out what the patient's symptoms are. Here we start seeing some differences among individual patients. In Reshma's case, the manifestations of MS were facial paralysis and blurred vision.

At a deeper level, we have emotions that accompany the symptoms. This is even more specific. In various individuals, the same condition may produce anxiety, anger, grief, suspicion, cheerfulness, excitement, violence and so on. In fact, there may be individuals who remain cheerful despite their problems.

However, when these emotions are investigated further, one can see that they arise from a specific *perception* of the situation. For example, the feeling of disappointment, sadness or rejection may arise in an individual from a sense of being forsaken or abandoned by close relations. He may even create a picture of this situation by saying he feels alone as in a desert. This perception of reality may explain a lot about the individual's way of seeing and reacting to situations. It is a kind of fixed perception, which I refer to as the level of delusion or imagination. This perception is most apparent in the crisis situations of an individual's life.

We can even explore this deeper and ask the patient how he experiences being in that situation or perception. For instance, how does it feel to be alone in the desert? It is at this point that the patient can go into his core experience, which may be one of terror or panic, and start experiencing the entire gamut of those feelings physically and emotionally.

The pattern of that experience actually defines who the individual is at his deepest level. We can identify which kingdom—plant, mineral or animal—is active within him at that moment. That experience could be one of sensitivity and reactivity, one of losing or lacking structure, or one of survival.

Sometimes, in a crisis moment or in a deeper exploration in case taking, the person can get in touch with the sensory experience or his core pattern, the sensation. This happened in Reshma's case nearly three years into her treatment.

She came to me one day for her follow-up, and she was visibly upset. A problem at her workplace had upset her a lot. It had something to do with her being sidestepped by another colleague, who was being sent abroad for an important meeting instead of her. When I asked how she felt about it (emotion), she described feelings of anger and sadness. Then I asked her how she perceived the situation. She said it was as though she had been pushed to a corner. As if there was less space for her (delusion/imagination).

Then I asked her to focus on this image of being pushed

to a corner and to allow the inner experience to come to her awareness. At that point she described it in the following words, 'It was like there was a big cloud on top of me and there was darkness. There was a pressure on the neck and I felt that clouds are enveloping me. There was lot of weight on the head, and the base of the neck, it felt very heavy.' She said she wanted to push back the weight but was not strong enough; she was trying to push it away and come out of it. The feeling of pressure and weight was felt throughout the body and also in her heart. This whole feeling created blankness and confusion.

In another part of her interview, when I asked her what she liked to do and not do, she said she did not like routine work, that there was no excitement in it, and that she wanted to feel charged up with lots of energy and movement. Her sensation was of lightness: 'As if you are a bubble that goes up in the air. I felt free and happy in that situation.'

What was interesting about Reshma was that although her emotional story was one of grief and rejection, at a far deeper level of perception and sensation there was a very simple and characteristic experience that emerged. On the one hand, there was a sensation of blackness, heaviness, being under a pressure, a weight and constriction, and on the other hand, she felt light, free and happy.

This very same sensation is clearly found in the plant subclass called *Hamamelididae*, which is the group to which cannabis belongs.

When she was describing darkness and heaviness, her

hands were moving down from above, showing the pressure she was experiencing. Through this gesture, she was expressing her inner sensation of heaviness and pressure. These sensations are typical of a particular plant of the *Hamamelididae* group.

I gave her a remedy from this group called *Fagus sylvatica.*

With this remedy, she has not had a relapse for the past four years. Her energy level improved significantly and overall, her energy to walk and exert herself improved a lot. Her mood swings, anxiety and stress dramatically declined. Her experience of heaviness and constriction had become significantly milder.

She told me, 'Six years ago it was a challenge for me to move about in the house, and I avoided stairs. Now I go for a walk after lunch and can climb up to 250 stairs at one go.'

The movement of Reshma's hands when she had described her sensation and experience showed the energy pattern within. This is the sixth level, energy. When a person is asked to describe the sensation he experiences, at some point he may start using hand movements, gestures or sounds. These are an expression of his deepest inner pattern. Such an energy pattern lies at the very basis of who we are and how we express ourselves.

The seventh level is the level in which the patient witnesses the experiences at the other preceding levels. We can live at any level in our day-to-day lives. We can live at the level of name, fact, emotions, delusion/imagination, a local, sensory experience, energy pattern or at the level of a witness.

A healthy individual will need to be at a different level of experience in different situations. For example, when we are buying a movie ticket, we need to be at the level of fact: you pay for the ticket and receive it. When we are expressing care for another person, we need to be at the level of emotions. When we watch a movie, we need to be at the level of imagination. When we are riding on a roller coaster, we need to be at the level of sensation. Thus, we need to change or be flexible with our levels of experience according to the circumstance. Most of us do not have that flexibility, and we tend to be more or less stuck at one level during a given period in our lives. The fixedness of the level we are at is a part of the unhealthy state.

During the case-taking process, the homeopath attempts to take the patient to the deepest level of experience possible because the deeper he goes, the more he can perceive the individuality of each patient. Then the remedy to be recommended becomes clearer. It is at the level of sensation that the homeopath can detect which kingdom is expressing itself. In follow-ups, I attempt to go deeper into the experience of the patient to see if the core experience remains the same.

Here is the transcript of a follow-up session I had with Reshma. She had come to see me just after another crisis had occurred at her workplace.

D: Describe your experience of this feeling of rejection and anger? How did you feel?

R: I felt angry at myself . . . it's something . . . I have a lot of questions. I feel a lot of question marks within myself. I ask myself why is this happening. All of these questions were centred on me attacking myself, questioning whether there is something wrong with me.

D: How do you experience the situation within you?

R: Inside it feels as if you are bound by some chains. These chains are large. These are iron chains and I am standing. There is darkness around me and there is also a light on me but I am bound by chains [here she showed both her fists facing and pushing towards each other]. You feel very constricted and I want to break through that.

D: Describe the word constricted.

R: Constricted means they are holding me. The chains are around my hands and the upper part of the body so I want to break them. I am putting a pressure from the inside to break that chain but that chain is not breaking. It is very strong.

D: How does it feel to be bound in chains and be constricted?

R: I don't feel helpless in that, I am trying to break that.

D: Trying?

41

R: Since there's a lot of pressure from inside, a lot of strength is needed.

D: Describe the sensation of constriction a little more. Use other words to describe that sensation.

R: There is a little difficulty in breathing at this point of time. When I feel constricted, I am trying to take lots of breaths, but the amount of oxygen that is coming in is less. I can move around but my hands cannot do what they are supposed to do and it is very frustrating at this point of time.

D: Describe constriction a little more. Use more words to describe that sensation.

R: I want freedom.

D: Describe freedom.

R: Freedom means you can do what you want to do.

D: What is the experience of freedom?

R: Freedom means there is lot of light, there is something like the sky, there is movement, there is action, there is a happiness there.

D: What is the experience within you of freedom?

R: It's very light-hearted. Very, very light, you feel like a bubble in the air. It goes wherever it has to go but it does what it is supposed to do. When I am saying freedom, it means whatever light is there inside of the body is getting utilized properly.

From here I could see that the sensations were still similar to those we saw earlier—an indication that I should stay with the same remedy, provided that it had helped. So I asked her some more questions.

D: Now tell me one thing—you came to me four years ago. How are you today as compared to four years ago?

R: Amazingly different, very different. When I came at that time, I was very helpless, I was very scared. I didn't know what was going to happen. I was worried about my future and had a lot of stress. You know, like whether I will be able to manage things or not. The more I would think and read about this disease, the more scared I used to be. Today I feel for the first time, I mean this happened a few days ago, I was able to talk to somebody and tell them that I have multiple sclerosis. I could not talk all these years. I think that is the difference. Whenever I read books on patients' stories, I think I am really lucky to be in this position here and I don't think I am a patient. That feeling of confidence is very strong.

During her moments of crisis, Reshma used to experience the sensation of heaviness. I asked her whether she had noticed a change in the intensity of this sensation as compared to earlier. She reported that the sensation was significantly diminished, and it was hardly 10 or 15 per cent of what it used to be.

She has continued to do very well on this remedy.

~

Each individual has his own sensitivity and reactivity, which is prevalent throughout his whole story and pervades all aspects of his life. That is the disease. That is the cause of stress. That is what needs to be perceived. That is what needs to be healed.

The discovery of the different levels, the deeper level of sensation, the differentiation of that deep experience into kingdoms and then further differentiation—all these are the new developments in homeopathy. Used along with traditional methods of symptom matching, they have added a very important dimension to homeopathic practice. These developments have also shown us what disease really is and where it arises from. That gives us more possibilities to become aware.

Awareness is the first step towards healing. The awareness referred to here is not an academic understanding or an inspection of a behaviour or thought pattern within ourselves. Nor is it a flash of realization or an interpretation by someone else. Awareness is a process. It is a process of going within oneself without the mind, and going into the depth of one's experience over and over again. It is a process that can begin now and extend over several months or years. It is a gradual awakening to one's inner world. It is a silent, non-verbal, non-cerebral process, where one can hear what *other song* is playing within and become aware of how it has shaped everything in one's life.

4

THE HOMEOPATHIC
PROCESS

The formally qualified homeopathic doctor possesses
knowledge of all medical sciences. He takes the case history,
examines the patient on a mental, emotional and physical
level, and gets the necessary medical investigations done.

However, the most important thing is the selection of
the homeopathic medicine. The patient requires one out of
a possible 4000 remedies. In order to select the right remedy,
the homeopath needs to fully understand the experience of
each individual patient.

As demonstrated earlier, in homeopathy, treatment
is based on precise details of the various symptoms from
which an individual patient suffers. It is not based merely
on the name of the disease or the diagnosis alone. A remedy
is selected by considering each and every detail, even some
of the minutest symptoms of the patient.

For example, it is not enough to simply say, 'I have a headache.' The homeopath requires much more precise detail in order to select a remedy. If the patient says, 'I have a headache which is worse on the left side in my temple and it feels like a sharp, shooting pain,' this description is more individualizing and can indicate a specific remedy to fit that specific symptom picture.

A homeopath aims to investigate each aspect of a complaint—what makes it better or worse, what accompanies the complaint, where exactly is it located, how does it feel, and so on. When investigating a patient, the homeopath must have a good understanding of who the patient is, his age, temperament, individuality, the nature of the disease and pathology. Symptoms that are specific, strange, rare and peculiar are often the most useful for the homeopath.

Even one symptom has several components that can make it complete from the homeopathic case-taking point of view. Each symptom of the patient should be examined thoroughly, with the aim to elicit all of the above-mentioned components and more. Similarly, we understand the patient as a whole or a totality through a number of components, such as childhood, crisis moments or stressful events, dreams, fears and so on. For reasons of comprehension, we see these different factors as separate, but they are all expressions of the same phenomenon.

For example, a person comes with the complaint of stiffness in the joints, which has started after a strain or over-lifting, which is aggravated at the beginning of motion and gets better by continued motion. We could analyse each part separately, but all of these parts are expressions of the same phenomenon, which indicates one homeopathic remedy.

After obtaining the above information, a search is made among homeopathic remedies; and through our tools, the repertories and the *Materia Medica*, we are able to find the one that most closely resembles the pattern of the disease of the patient.

When a patient approaches a homeopath, the homeopath first observes how the person enters, how he walks and how he talks. After listening to the narrative of the complaint, the homeopath examines all its aspects. A great deal of attention is paid to where the complaint is located, what the sensation is, what makes it better or worse, and what accompanies the problem. What is also essential to know is the effect the problem has on the life of the patient.

After this, the homeopath might look into various areas in the patient's life that point to the individuality of the patient. What were his most stressful events or crisis moments? How did he perceive and react to them? What are his dreams like? What are his interests and hobbies? How was his childhood?

Through all these aspects the homeopath is able to see a connecting thread of the patient's experience in each of these situations. That experience, known as the 'core experience' or 'sensation' of the patient, is then analysed in finer detail. One must understand: is it an experience of survival, sensitivity or loss of structure/performance? This understanding, along with the particular symptoms of the patient, is used to select an appropriate remedy.

As homeopaths, our primary intention is to help our patients get well in the most gentle yet rapid way. In order to help our patients we rely on their cooperation, as the medicine we prescribe is selected mainly on the basis of the symptoms they reveal to us. It is important that we are able to understand all the features that belong to our patients as individuals, their reactions to various factors, including their main problem, their past and present family history, and mental make-up. We are then able to make a successful prescription that aids us in removing the ailment. The medicine not only works on the symptoms but also on the person as a whole.

In order to extract the maximum information from our patients, we ask a number of questions. Each of these questions has a definite meaning and significance for us. Not a single question is useless. Even something that a patient may feel is not connected with his problem may be the most important factor in deciding the correct homeopathic medicine. It is important for patients to be free and frank, and give the fullest possible information on each aspect of their lives.

The case has to be taken tactfully, correctly and completely.

The important symptoms have to be elicited and quickly recognized from all the possible details. Homeopathic case taking involves a great deal of artistry and paying close attention to the individuality of the patient.

The areas of fears, first impression, dreams, childhood, interests and hobbies, lifestyle, crisis situations, etc., are very important to examine because they all tie in together to help us to discover the other song in each individual.

If you take each of these aspects a step further, you come to a common experience, which is the underlying experience of all these aspects. It is that common experience which points to the main experience or the kingdom to which the patient belongs. This is the most fascinating thing to learn in a case.

Psychiatrists talk at the level of the mind. Homeopathy takes it to a much deeper level. It connects the mind to the body, and, finally, the human being to nature. We have to understand the underlying experience that is the centre of each patient. This centre is the same for all the above-mentioned aspects. When you come to that point, you can see the song playing within.

This book tells the story of the homeopathic process mainly through the case studies of three individuals—Bharat, Dr Ali and Chetan. Through their stories and their healing, one can learn valuable lessons about oneself. We will travel with each of them through the various aspects of their lives. Through investigating their main problems, their childhood, different crisis situations, relationships, dreams, fears and so on, we will discover the individual, unique golden thread which runs through their lives.

As we travel through this book and through the case studies, we will see examples and explanations for each kingdom (plant, mineral and animal), the respective sensations, and discover the innermost experience of each patient. Through an exhaustive study of each case, we will see the similarities and contrasts between each inner song, reaction pattern and deepest experience. We will explore how each case was analysed homeopathically, through symptoms as well as kingdoms. We will also see follow-ups of what happened after the homeopathic remedy was given. If this book helps you to turn your attention inward and to examine your experience, pattern of behaviour and sensory experiences in various situations, it will have served its purpose.

5

FIRST IMPRESSIONS

The homeopathic *Materia Medica* is extremely detailed in its observation, and so should a homeopath be when observing and understanding a patient. For instance, the homeopath asks the patient about his past illness and he replies, 'I had typhoid,' and then is unsure whether he had typhoid eight or twelve years ago. In sorting out his confusion about the time, he inadvertently scratches just above his right ear. This simple detail is an indication for the remedy. In the repertories, the symptom reads: 'confusion, scratches above the right ear'.

The homeopath trains himself to observe all these minute behaviours and characteristics of the patient, right from the moment the person takes an appointment and walks into his office. First impressions are formed not only when the homeopath sees the patient for the first time, but include what is observed before he visits the clinic. There is always a kind of preamble, a kind of preview of how he comes. For example:

— Who refers him?
— With what urgency?
— With what kind of hope or doubt?
— With what kind of attitude? Is he desperate, mild or demanding?

And then the observations of his entry into the clinic:

— How does he walk in?
— Is he alone?
— Is he accompanied by someone else? If so, what is the relation and interaction like between the two?

All these questions are vital to understanding the patient, initially at the most superficial and surface level. I have seen cases where the accompanying person speaks for the patient through the entire case. I have seen children who know the answer, but whisper it to the mother to convey it to me. It reminds me of the case of a very quiet woman from Kerala. She arrived at the clinic accompanied by her husband. She did not respond to my greeting, sat beside her husband, and allowed him to begin the consultation.

After their marriage fifteen years ago, they had settled in Mumbai. Recently, his wife had become very fearful. She was too afraid to sleep alone at night when he was away on a trip. The husband informed me: 'Doctor, in the last few months, she even calls our thirteen-year-old son at night to share her room. She is too afraid to be alone.'

I turned to her and asked if there had been any kind

of stress in her life after which these fears emerged. She glanced towards her husband and he continued to speak for her. 'Well, yes. She was very affected by the loss of her friend, a neighbour who lived in our building. After her friend's death, she started to become frightened, especially of sleeping alone.'

What can we understand from this? We could look at the symptom in the repertories: 'Ailments from death of parents or friends'. This is a direct choice. We have taken the exact information and circumstance described by the patient's husband and looked into the repertories, basing our choice on a single situation.

If we take one step further and ask ourselves 'Why is she *so* affected by the death of her friend? Who is she? Who reacts to the loss of a friend in this way?' we may come to a fuller understanding of the totality of her expression.

I tried again to engage her and simply asked, 'Tell me something about yourself.'

Her eyes quickly darted towards her husband and once more he responded: 'She was born and lived most of her life in Kerala. We came to live in Bombay fifteen years ago, but she still does not have any friends here. In our entire apartment complex, she had only one friend. So when that lady passed away, it was a huge loss.'

As her husband continued the story, I understood that the neighbour was also born in Kerala and spoke the same language as the woman, which had brought the two together. They spent hours talking, going to the market, sharing recipes and, when the husband was travelling, this neighbour was always available for support in case of any emergency.

Interestingly, in her fifteen years of living in Mumbai, our patient had not tried to learn either of the local languages, Hindi or Marathi, and she certainly had not attempted to learn English. The only person she could converse with outside the family was her friend, and this made her death a huge loss indeed.

Who was the neighbour to the patient? What had she lost? What did this tell us about her? The patient depended heavily on her neighbour for support since moving to Mumbai—just as she sat in the consultation room, saying hardly a word, and totally depending on her husband to describe her problem.

When I attempted to engage her directly in the conversation, there was a childish quality in her dependence on her husband. When he was away, she depended on her son, as if she were a child who needed someone to lean on for support. From this, we can take the symptom: childish behaviour. This characterized her general state. We can also take the symptom: weeping and tearful mood, as if she had no friends.

The remedy coming through these rubrics is *Baryta carbonica* (see also chapter 12, n. 1).

In *Baryta carbonica*, there is a childish dependence, stemming from a feeling of inability to learn new things, like a new language, or the inability to adapt to new circumstances and take on new responsibilities. This leads to a reserved, inferior, timid feeling, as if everyone is a stranger and the patient is alone. We can also look for the symptom 'aggravation in the presence of strangers', which reflects the inner feeling of *Baryta carbonica*.

In this way homeopaths need to understand both the patients and their symptoms. We need to go *behind* the symptom which is manifest, deeper into the experience of the patient's life. We need to acquire a fuller understanding of our patient to grasp the underlying perception and then carefully choose symptoms that reflect the whole.

Soon after taking *Baryta carbonica*, our patient's fear of sleeping alone completely disappeared. But it was six months after the initial consultation when my heart marvelled at the power of homeopathy. She arrived for her follow-up unescorted and talked to me in Hindi for a few minutes.

There are many other things that go into first impressions. I have even observed simple things, like when you ask a patient a question, they may repeat the question back to you or say, 'I don't know what to say, you guide me.'

The first sentence they speak is very important; for example, I had a patient who came to me and the first thing he said was, 'You're the last hope'. This exhibits the level of desperation or expectation of the patient. Also important is how they dress, walk, talk, speak with the receptionist, and so on.

Once there was a woman who had taken an appointment

for 9 a.m. Unfortunately, an emergency case came up just before that, and I told my assistant to begin the case taking; after handling the acute situation, I would see the woman. After twenty minutes, the assistant came and told me that the patient had become very upset and appeared to be very angry. Luckily, I had just finished with my acute case, so I called her in. I could see she was indeed very, very angry. She was glaring at me though she was not saying much. I told her that homeopathy is based upon understanding a person, and that during a crisis a person's real state of being comes to the surface. Right at that moment, she was in her true state, so I asked her if she was okay going with me into that experience of her state, to which she agreed. This was the moment when she was experiencing her sensation at its peak, which was also a good time to explore it further.

She said, 'I am so angry, I felt as if I had been made a guinea pig, as if I had been exposed, denuded, stripped, and it is injustice that you are experimenting with me. Sending me to the assistant and student—what kind of experiment is this?—I am so angry. It is injustice.' I asked her the experience of this, and she said, 'I would just like to lash out, but I cannot. You are my doctor and it is wrong to vent out anger at the doctor.'

So this was the first impression of how I saw her. From that very moment, I could see a kind of split in her mind, between the need to lash out at perceived injustice and undeserved suffering, and on the other hand, she told herself she couldn't do it because it would be wrong.

This gave me the clue to her remedy: *Naja*.[1]

One religious leader, whom I visited, was surrounded by a number of his followers and devotees. As such, it was very difficult to take his case. Any question I would ask, he would answer with another question. For example, if I asked him, 'What do you like in food and drink?' he would answer, 'Does a yogi have any preferences? Does a yogi differentiate between one thing and another? No, everything is the same for the yogi ...' and so forth. Any question I would ask, I would get a reply in the form of another question, often a rhetorical one.

I was tempted to ask him why he answered every question of mine with another question, but I kind of knew that the answer would probably be, 'Why not?' This observation led me to the symptom: 'Questions speak, continuously in'. That gave me his remedy: *Aurum metallicum*.[2]

Once a lady came to my office, and there was a delay in seeing her. The resident doctor came hurriedly to me and said, 'The next patient is making a lot of noise in the reception area because she's having to wait for fifteen–twenty minutes. If we don't call her in for consultation, she's saying she will leave.'

This was unusual, because people are used to waiting for an hour or more, particularly in a doctor's office. Moreover, we'd already told her it would take two hours for the whole process, so she should not have made another appointment so soon after.

I wrapped up the previous consultation and called

her inside. When we started talking, I realized she was in no hurry at all. She had not looked at her watch even once. It was obvious she had no other appointment scheduled. Then, when describing her nature, she said, 'It is very important for me to be occupied all the time by something. If I'm not occupied, I feel very bored. This boredom is what I simply cannot stand. So, all the time I find some kind of entertainment to keep me occupied, in order to avoid the boredom which causes me a lot of pain and suffering.'

That was the reason why she had made a scene and wanted to be called in immediately. The homeopathic remedy *Piper nigrum*,[3] which is made out of black pepper, has exactly that experience of blandness and boredom with the opposite sensation of excitement and entertainment.

Another reference we consider in first impressions is the case record form. The case record form is an extensive questionnaire aiming to gain insight into all areas of the life of the patient. Some people fill out the form and some people don't fill it out at all. Some are meticulous about it—sometimes apologetic even if they have filled it out perfectly—while some are totally indifferent.

Then, of course, there are subtle, non-verbal dynamics that one can sense from the beginning of the interaction. For example, some patients give off a feeling of extreme fragility, as though they are saying, 'I am very sensitive, treat me with gloved hands . . .' With these kinds of people, you have to be overcautious. There was once a gentleman who came to the clinic and the first thing he said was, 'Doctor, please don't give me strong medicine because my whole system reacts badly to it. You know, other people may take it, no problem. But my system cannot take it. I can only take a little, much less than others, so please don't give me a medicine that's too strong. My system cannot handle it.'

For a homeopath, this is the peculiarity of the patient. This symptom is not directly available in the repertories, but it is an important characteristic of the patient. What is next? Let us try to understand what he was expressing.

He did not say merely that the medicine was strong, but that *his system* could not handle it, which was not as sturdy as other people's systems. So, it was like saying, 'Be careful with me, I am delicate. I am not tough. I could break.' This is the exact feeling of the homeopathic medicine reflected in the repertories as a mental symptom: when the body parts are considered delicate. This is a common request from a *Thuja* patient. This is the main quality of the conifer plant family, expressed through the patient's sensation of 'brittleness'.

Furthermore, when they first come in, some patients can be very attention-seeking, as though they are screaming out 'Look at me!' or those who try to occupy the doctor in engaging conversation or through dramatic gestures. Some are reticent, while others talk non-stop! The art in homeopathy is what the homeopath is able to see, hear and perceive beyond the verbal responses given by the patient. Detailed observation and listening skills are keys to success.

The physical appearance of the patient, too, is important. His face, build, gait, manner of sitting and speaking are essential to who he is as a person. How he enters the room can also give some vital clues.

Once there was a very dramatic case, in which a woman came to my clinic and stopped dead in the doorway. As a regular practice, I record sessions with patients to be able to use them as a teaching guide. She looked at the video camera, pointed a finger at it while still standing in the doorway of my consulting room, and said, 'If you insist on recording my case, I do not want to take your treatment.'

The manner in which she said it was aggressive and intended to intimidate. I was intrigued about her reaction. Of course, some other patients also refuse the recording, but not in such a direct and aggressive manner. They might do it more politely and say simply that they do not want to be recorded.

I made her sit down, and asked her if I could just record the audio, and she agreed. I asked her what the feeling was behind her not wanting to be on video. She said, 'I don't want anyone to know anything about me which I don't want them to know. Even if it is a small thing such as I like sweets.' She expanded further, 'It is okay for me if an unknown person comes to know, but if a known person will have some information about me, I would feel very threatened. It is as if this information could be used against me somewhere.'

This feeling had dominated her whole life. She had

always remained in the shadows, not coming out in the open because of these fears.

A very interesting aspect of her case was when I asked about her interests and hobbies. She mentioned that the stories of the holocaust fascinated her. She was very sensitive to the fact that the Jewish people were betrayed in Nazi Germany by the people who knew them closely. She would almost experience going through the horror of it, even though she has absolutely no connection with Germans or the Jewish people, as she had been born and raised in India.

The remedy that helped her immensely was *Hyoscyamus niger*.[4] It is worth noting that a year or so into her treatment, she had no objections to being recorded on video. She had even forgotten that she had initially had such a severe objection.

What is particularly important is the consistency in the case. What a homeopath sees should corroborate with what he hears. Just making a list of observations about the person is not enough. While observing, a homeopath has to hear both what the person is saying and how he's saying it, simultaneously noting down his main complaints. Homeopaths have to be very alert and take special note that all the expressions of the person are corresponding with each other.

Starting with their first impressions, let us meet the three people whom we will be joining on their homeopathic journey.

BHARAT

Bharat walked into my room. He was very thin and lean and wore a woollen sweater, even though the temperature outside wasn't so cold. He spoke very little, in a low, nearly inaudible monotone, and seemed very frightened. I knew he was thirty-five from his case record form, but he appeared quite young, meek and scared. His face was bony and hollow, and the expression tense and serious.

I asked him why he was looking so nervous. He explained that he had just come in a taxi. When he got out after making the payment, he had an altercation with the driver about the change that was due to him. He got scared, and thought that somehow the driver would follow and harm him. Now his fear was making him tremble and causing palpitations.

When I glanced at his case record form, I saw that he had extensively typed out everything. He had even colour-coordinated the text, stating which colour had more importance than the next. He coloured the questions in green; the most important information was in blue and bold; and the lesser important information remained black. I gave him some time to calm down before asking him what had brought him to me.

DR ALI

Dr Ali was a man in his sixties, and his complaint was obvious, as his entire face and most of his body was covered in eczema. Dr Ali had filled out his case record form in the most beautiful handwriting I had ever seen—which bordered on being calligraphic. He had even corrected the cover of the form by adding the address of my clinic, and on the first page, he had written a short and poetic quote.

Grass grows by inches
And dies by feet...

At the back of the form, in the three blank pages meant for the patient to write his complaints, Dr Ali had filled the space with his poetry (see pp. 64–65). The poems, most of them haikus and tankas, were written in esoteric language, in which every other word had to be looked up in the dictionary.

From the way the form was presented to me, naturally my first question was about his poetry rather than his eczema. The professor was more than happy to elaborate. There were two qualities that were the most notable about his explanation. The first was his very deep and confident voice, not unlike that of a newsreader's. The second was the deliberate way in which he framed sentences, and the choice of complex words. His pride in explaining each word was apparent, almost as though he were teaching poetry. It was a long time before we even started talking about his problem.

HAIKU

*

Grown, children have flown.
A songbird has adopted
Now my empty nest

*

My heart at last stopped.
Its unremitting ticking
No more disturbs sleep

*

Newfangled steroids
Sex up the broads' embonpoint:
Wives remain virgins

(overleaf...)

*

Water burns the skin,
Doctors are no fire fighters.
Eczema is rage

*

Grief – a soloist
Shuns the band of solace and
Camaraderie

*

Two mobike trips to
The mountains. Four young riders.
Only one tomb. Me

*

What recks thy broad brow
Messiah? The blight of pain
On the Tree of Life

— x — x —

CHETAN

Many years ago, I was asked to judge a debating competition at a local college in Mumbai. The debate was on whether or not intuition exists. After a few students had their turn, another name was announced. A voice was heard on the speakers: 'Can you see me?' Everyone was looking at the stage but no one could be seen. Again, the voice spoke: 'Can you all see me? What about now?' Still there was no face to the voice.

The voice continued: 'Does intuition really exist and can it be proven that it exists?' This voice obviously was pro-intuition. As he walked on to the stage into the plain view of the audience, Chetan confidently said, 'That is how intuition is: you cannot see it, but some can hear it, some can feel it, and most experience it.'

What an entrance! Needless to say, the whole crowd was impressed.

Chetan, as I learnt later, had been very active in the political and social scene at his college. He had been on the student council at a senior position and was considered popular. He liked this kind of attention. He was obviously good at public speaking and debating, and was quite dramatic in his endeavours.

The most interesting part for me during the case taking was his hurried manner of speaking. There was also a rapid movement of his hands at all times. Literally at no point in the case was he not waving about his hands. He would lift his hand in the air, palm facing downward, and rock it from side to side, very quickly in a fluttering motion. He used many other emphatic hand gestures as well.

6

OBSERVING THE LANGUAGE OF THE PATIENT

As mentioned before, in homeopathy, the patient's language or way of communication, both verbal and non-verbal, is vital to understanding their innermost feelings and experiences, and gives an indication of their unique inner patterns.

We aim to link body language (non-verbal) with what is spoken (verbal language) to read a symptom in its totality. This kind of analysis requires attentive vision, a high level of expertise and sustained observation.

Verbal Language

Homeopathic doctors must be very attuned to a patient's verbal language. Verbal communication is the main way of conveying messages face-to-face. Among the key components of the verbal communication are words, sound, speaking and language.

What language the patient uses, what words he chooses to describe his experience, what volume, tone and pitch of the voice he uses, at what speed he speaks, how clearly, and the overall type of speech are all indicative of a patient's individuality.

All these factors of voice and speech can reflect many psychological aspects of a person. For example, someone who's angry may stammer or speak in a high-pitched tone. Someone who's depressed or nervous will speak in a monotone or low voice. Does the patient speak loudly and rapidly? Does he have a clear, controlled and steady voice? Is he very talkative, bubbly and jumps from subject to subject? Is the patient mumbling, stammering, moaning or sighing? How does the patient laugh or weep? Is it loud? Is it prolonged? Does laughing alternate with crying?

Verbal communication is an irreplaceable resource for observing feelings, ideas and experiences. There are different ways in which the patient speaks, depending on his or her own inner experience. In the earlier chapters, we saw that the three main categories of experience are Sensitivity, Structure and Competition. Each has its own set of key words and phrases, representative of that experience. Let's look at each of them in detail.

Sensitivity and Reactivity (Plant Kingdom)

In people whose primary experience is sensitivity and reactivity, it all comes down to things that 'affect' them. These people may not directly say they are sensitive, but it is conveyed and implied when they say, 'I am affected by this, that or the other.' For example, someone who has a pattern of sensitivity and reactivity might say, 'Mumbai is okay, except for the poverty. This affects me.' What he is meaning to say is that Mumbai per se is not an issue, but he is sensitive to the poverty.

When patients of the plant kingdom present their complaints to the homeopath, they will seem haywire, rounded, wandering, descriptive, and the symptoms will be described randomly and incompletely. These individuals prefer flowery, irregular patterns, something that appeals to their aesthetic sensitivity. Their writing, too, is in irregular patterns, usually rounded and disorganized. Even though they present their complaints in a disorganized fashion, with their acute sensitivity they feel most things intensely and are very elaborate in their descriptions.

Structure and Function (Mineral Kingdom)

In individuals whose primary experience is structure and function, there is a feeling of something lacking in them, something that will go missing or has been lost. These people see something wrong with themselves, and experience a problem within. It is a fear, a lack or a loss of something within. Common examples include: 'I may lose my voice', 'I fear being paralysed and unable to walk', 'My back is very weak, I need a support for my back', etc. All these examples reveal that the lack, loss or fear is from within.

The speech of these individuals is to the point. It is very uniform, structured and organized. When they present their complaints, they present it in an organized, structured way, with numbers, percentages and calculations, systematically and methodically, with precision.

Competition and Survival (Animal Kingdom)

In people whose deepest experience is one of competition and survival, they perceive things as 'me versus you', 'me versus the other person', or even 'me versus myself'. In these individuals, it is other human beings who affect them. For example, 'He is bad', 'He is the problem', 'I am better than him', 'I will beat them to get to the very top'.

These individuals speak in an attention-seeking manner, they get excited and animated, their descriptions are vivid and full of life, and they speak at a moderate to fast speed. When they present their complaints, it is done with a lot of feeling, in an animated style. They try to hold the attention of the homeopath. Their eyes are alert and they make a lot of eye contact.

Non-Verbal Cues

Non-verbal cues such as a person's gait, posture, body

language, and so on, are as important to the homeopath as to anyone else who wants to know more about that person.

Observation of children's actions is especially important as they reveal their individuality. I had this child as a patient who sat on his mother's lap and kept his head buried in her shoulder, glancing at me occasionally. Whenever I looked at him, he would hide his face behind her shoulder. It was as though he wanted to be noticed and appreciated, but at the same time felt embarrassed and bashful. This became the starting point of my inquiry process.

There was another child who constantly moved all around the room—he would not sit still for a moment—and kept changing his activity. He would colour with crayons for a few minutes, then go and open the drawer, and then shift again to another place. Whenever he moved, it was to indulge in an activity, but it was only for a few minutes each.

Another kind of child could be very friendly and come close, even communicate with the homeopath, and observe his every action.

These kinds of observations help immensely in knowing the individual. However, there is one thing that certain homeopaths have begun to use, especially in recent times, which is probably not utilized that often by others—and that is the hand gestures.

When we delve further into a person's feelings, there is a point at which he goes to a level of experience that is deeper than that of the mind. For example, the patient may say that he feels an anxiety in a specific situation. When we ask for the experience of the anxiety or how it is felt, at that point he cannot express it in words because that experience is both physical and mental. It could be a certain feeling of choking, tightness, stiffness or suffocation, but it is no one word that can describe it—it is a whole experience. At that moment, to express that experience, the patient starts using his hand gestures. The expression becomes non-verbal. With certain gestures, sounds and movements of his body, he is able to describe that experience.

The homeopath observes this expression very carefully and uses it as the starting point for the exploration into the patient's inner experience. He makes the patient focus on that gesture or body movement which expresses his experience. This allows him to go deeper into himself.

When a person uses gestures repeatedly, the adage 'actions speak louder than words' becomes true. Hand gestures are subconscious, involuntary, and are often not even noticed by the individual making them. They unconsciously reveal their inner experience. It is very helpful if the homeopath makes the patient focus on that gesture and sees what comes up in the patient's experience.

For example, one of my patients, a young schoolgirl, said that she felt very bad when her friends did not share everything with her. When asked to elaborate, she initially kept describing it as feeling bad, sad or depressed, but all the while her hands were flying in the air. This was the same hand gesture that she used while describing her headache. She explained, 'It is like something is being forced out!' This was also the experience with her friends—that they, through their actions, were somehow forcing her out, leaving her aside to the point of exclusion. Here we see the meaning of the gesture on both a physical and mental–emotional level.

In another case, the person described her asthmatic attacks as a sensation of the upper chest being tightly twisted, like being choked and strangled. The image for the sensation was that of a python strangling its prey. Later on in the case she spoke of being hurt when her husband admonished her. When I asked her to describe this feeling of hurt, she used the word sad, while her clenched hands went towards her chest. This was the same gesture she had used when describing a strangled, twisted feeling in the chest. What her words could not capture, her hands expressed, without her even being conscious of it.

The gesture becomes like a secret door or a hidden passage into the land of the person's experiences. What is the language, both verbal and non-verbal, of our three sample patients?

BHARAT

In the case of Bharat, from his entrance into the clinic, we saw he was withdrawn and unwilling to speak. I could barely hear his low voice. His eyes, beneath a furrowed brow, told me that he was terrified, and they were staring at me.

Looking closely at his case record form, I observed Bharat's aggressive speech. To the question 'How long do you remember hurts caused to you by others?' he wrote: 'Sticks like glue and I remember them forever. When my father was alive, the only thing I wanted to do was to torture, beat and break him into tiny bits and pieces and kill him.'

He also explained in the case form that over the phone everyone thinks he is a girl or woman.

DR ALI

In the case of Dr Ali, we had noted that his voice was deep and confident and he spoke in elegantly formed sentences, verging on the poetic. He was extremely well spoken and had a proficient command of English.

See Dr Ali's case form for more examples of his language. In the Appetite and Thirst section he wrote:

I am not a gourmet or a gastronome. I eat in order to exist. I can subsist for months on scraps or leftovers of dishes. I eat thrice a day at fixed hours. I can manage to go hungry for long, I don't like munching or browsing in between. I have a lot of thirst, as I ascribe it to the talking of the profession, teaching.

A few excerpts from the blank pages are:

Some observations about my personality (persona, mask, character, identity, dissimilation):

Drifted away (mentally) from family, kith and kin, clan, religion, nationhood, terrestrial affinity. Feel like an incorrigible gypsy. I am never at home any place, anywhere. I want to move on, with the grimy slugs on my shoulder.

Was conventionally religious, but slowly drifted away from dogma, ethnicity, faith. Have been a vocal iconoclast and an agnostic. . . .

Was a nocturnal creature for over a quarter century. Loved loafing around, studying, listening to music throughout the night.

Have been a freak case of study through four media. Was an ordinary mediocre back-bencher till the eighth standard.

Across the career graph I excelled in Urdu, Persian, Hindi and English. Have a working knowledge of Gujarati, Marathi, Kacchi, and Hindustani. Am an amateur linguist and lexicographer, I can point out mistakes, slips, mispronunciations in a standard dictionary.

CHETAN

The first impression I had of Chetan was his majestic entrance into the lecture hall. Although his speech was hurried, he displayed confidence and creativity during the debate. He had a dramatic flare and spoke clearly and assuredly.

During his case taking I noticed his non-verbal cues more. His restlessness and excessive hand gesturing were two that stood out. For us as homeopaths, these objective and observable symptoms are vital clues for a patient's treatment.

~

It is very important for a homeopath to have peripheral vision, which can also be called tangential thinking. This refers to a homeopath's ability to not only follow the direct line of what the person is telling them, but also to simultaneously be able to take in information from the peripheral details that he mentions. Sometimes, the information that the homeopath takes in with his peripheral vision is more important than what the patient intends to convey.

For example, when I asked a patient about her cravings and aversions, she said she eats only vegetarian food. However, she belonged to a culture of essentially meat eaters. When asked the reason for her vegetarianism, it emerged that she was sensitive to the idea of killing and cruelty to animals. So, when asking about cravings, she talked about something in her nature that was individual to her. This kind of spontaneous revelation is more important and more characteristic.

This can be described by the word 'serendipity', which means that you find something you're not expecting to, while looking for something else. This is an important aspect of case taking. To reiterate, the homeopath is always looking for the consistency between the person's disease, what he says and what the homeopath personally sees. Many times the observation about the person corresponds with his choice of profession, with his hobbies and interests, and with his dreams. Everything has to come together.

7

THE PROBLEM

The chief complaint, or the problem the person comes to a homeopath with, is usually significant in terms of what it means to the individual and what it does to him. The symptoms of the chief complaint can give the homeopath an indication of a specific remedy. This includes the details of the physical location and exact sensation of the complaint, what makes it better or worse, and what accompanies it. For example, if a patient has severe abdominal pain, and the pain is of a colicky and spasmodic nature, which is made better by bending forward at the waist or raising your knees up to the abdomen, this is an indication of a particular remedy that may help. If the pain is a sharp, stitch-like pain, aggravated by the slightest movement, this is an indication for another medicine.

It is important that the homeopathic remedy is not prescribed based on only one view. It is based on other aspects, including the patient's nature, fears, dreams, hobbies and interests, as well as his reactions to various factors such as heat, cold, eating and drinking. For women, their menstrual pattern is also an aspect of the remedy picture.

The remedy has to match everything, both the physical complaints and the mental–emotional picture of the patient. The chief complaint often provides the most striking symptoms and can be a starting point for selecting the remedy. When homeopaths use primarily the characteristics of the chief complaint to decide the remedy, it is considered the traditional approach.

With the new approach, termed the sensation method and kingdom approach, to get an understanding of the deep experiences of the person, the chief complaint becomes even more important.

Through the sensation method, my colleagues and I discovered that investigating the experience of the chief complaint is the primary way to understand the patient's experience as a whole. What we do is aim to delve into the patient's experience of his complaint, which may be physical or emotional. The complaint can be pain, itching, breathlessness, a headache, or even emotional anxiety. We ask the patient how he experiences his complaint.

We subtly use open-ended questioning because it does not limit the patient's answer. It allows the patient to experience the problem at that very moment and to narrate the experience in the most accurate way possible.

This experience can frequently be illogical, strange and very individual. What is quite surprising is how each individual experiences the same illness or disease in a completely distinct way.

A young twenty-four-year-old woman limped painfully into my clinic one day with a very swollen knee. Her face contorted with pain as she eased herself into the chair. I could see how excruciating the pain was as she hobbled into my office. She could hardly walk. Immediately on sitting down she said, 'I am afraid! I am afraid of losing my leg, that they will amputate my leg!' Repeating her words, I asked, 'Tell me about losing your leg, about amputating your leg.'

She looked down and was very quiet for a moment. Then she said, 'Sometimes I have dreams of losing my father.' I was quite surprised by her spontaneous leap into the world of dreams from recounting her fears. I encouraged her to say more about how she felt in her dreams.

'I feel very, very anxious in the dream. I have many dreams where I feel so anxious. In one dream, I am working in a bank counting money. I am so, so careful, counting each stack of bills again and again. I know that if I make a mistake, they will take the money from my account and I will lose everything.'

Everywhere in this young woman's narration, I could hear anxiety about losing things: losing her leg, losing her father, losing money.

I continued the exploration. I asked, 'What are your plans for the future?'

She replied, surprisingly adamantly, 'One thing's for sure, I do not want to get married. I have heard so many stories where the girl gets married and after some time the husband says, "I don't want you any more," and the whole thing is lost. I never want to be in that situation ever! I am happy with my parents. I don't want a relationship that is unstable. From what I've seen, marriage is unstable and most often relationships end up being lost.'

Again, in each area of her life, I heard the same expression. Everywhere, there was the experience of loss and instability, the core expression repeating itself again and again.

When every expression of the patient comes to the same core sensation, to the same central experience, then we can be sure of our understanding. For this woman, the cause of stress was the fear that things are not stable. She feared that her knee joints were unstable; that her father, on whom she depended, could pass away; that money could be lost; and that any marital relationship was bound to end. All support systems were unstable and could let her down. With this insight, I looked for the symptom 'fear of poverty'.

The remedy I chose for her was *Calcarea fluorica*, which is a remedy for the treatment of bones, joints and especially the knee joints. Mentally and emotionally, anxiety and fear are also a part of the deepest experience of individuals needing this medicine.

After taking this remedy, the pain and swelling on

her knees reduced dramatically. She stayed off any other treatment and continued to improve. Within six months, her knee joint was as good as new and she was walking about freely. But the story doesn't end there. A few months later, she also accepted a marriage proposal! She is now married and lives contentedly with her husband and children in Mumbai.

To take another example, one patient came to me with a migraine. When I asked her about her experience of the headache, she described it to me saying, 'The headache is as if something is pulling inside. It is a sensation of something pulling inside and then it closes, and then it goes out of reach from the outside world.' This experience of something withdrawing and shutting itself in turned out to be her general experience in life. She perceived a threat from the outside world. She had actually 'shut herself up, into her own shell', The remedy I gave her not only healed her headaches but also changed her perception of life. She came out of her shell and was able to live like any other healthy person.

Similarly, when a person describes anxiety as a chief complaint, we are not merely interested in what causes the anxiety. Anxiety can arise from many places, such as fear of disease, the future, or of narrow, closed spaces. What the homeopath needs to find out is not only the cause or the aggravating factor, but also what the unique experience of the anxiety is.

I once treated a man in his mid-thirties whose main

problem was hoarseness in the voice. He had been advised surgery because they had found nodules in his vocal cords. He was a performer—a singer and a voice artist. The doctors told him that after the surgery he wouldn't be able to use his voice for a few weeks, and that's what made him seek out a homeopath.

When I asked him to describe his complaint, he said that, 'This loss of voice happens quite suddenly. I am singing or saying something and, all of a sudden, it is as if something comes from below, and my voice stops. It is out of the blue, something suddenly pops up which is quite threatening.'

This was a strange description, so I asked him to tell me more. 'It seems as if there are two people within me; one who is seen externally and the other is someone else who is hidden below. At times, this hidden person puts on an appearance most unexpectedly.'

Later in his treatment, when I asked him about what it is that he is sensitive to in events and news, the issue which he was most sensitive to, was terrorists. He described a terrorist as 'someone who came up unexpectedly, and can cause large amounts of damage. If I could get my hands on one, I would like to chop off his limbs while he is still alive.'

His whole state was of sensitivity to something coming up unexpectedly, to cause damage. This something was unseen and hidden. This set of qualities, which included the duality within himself, a sensitivity to something hidden below which emerges suddenly, like the idea of terrorism where this unseen, disguised, camouflaged force suddenly attacks with disastrous consequences, and, finally, the idea of being limbless, all fall into a pattern, which I could recognize as one from the snake group.

This patient did very well on a popular homeopathic snake remedy, *Lachesis*.[1]

Now let us examine each of our three patients' main complaints or problems, and the different nature and presentation of their complaints.

BHARAT

When I asked Bharat what had brought him to me, there was a long pause. Finally he said:

> I have problems with sleeping and I tend to be in a serious mood. Then the next moment I am ready to cry. I am very sensitive. A state of apathy. I am constantly agitated inside and I feel sad all the time. I get frustrated and feel uncomfortable all the time. It is like a tight feeling, as if I have some kind of injury, something being stuffed inside my head. Something big is forced into me and I am bearing it. It is like a pain. I am tired all the time, work is very difficult, and I have so much pain in the head. Overall it is a kind of numb feeling. Like the whole thing is numb. Like I am not aware of what is happening.

As the case taking progressed, I found that Bharat was severely depressed. He was suicidal and had tried all kinds of treatment to cure himself. He had had a variety of antidepressants, and he also had tried homeopathy in the past. His other complaints included unsteady hands and fingers, poor concentration and memory, exhaustion and tiredness.

He was a bachelor but was asocial. He did not have any friends, and he had never had a relationship with a woman before. He had no interest in life, and felt like a complete misfit. At one point in his life he had also tried committing suicide.

As mentioned before, his case record form had been neatly typed and the most important parts were highlighted in different colours. Below are excerpts from the chief complaint section:

I don't get sleep (this is my biggest and a long-standing complaint and it affects my life the most). It's a huge struggle and a luxury to get sleep. I toss and turn in bed continuously for several hours. And if I manage to eventually fall asleep, it is light sleep and is full of dreams. When I awake I feel so tired and exhausted, like I have just returned from war or a battlefield. Sometimes during my sleep, towards the end I would say when I am sleeping, I experience numbness . . . I won't be able to breathe . . . I am terrified, not able to move any part of my body, and I will be choking. It's like everything is coming to an end. I am always exhausted and tired. I always feel very weak like I don't have energy. . . .

I experience constant brooding, like having been badly hurt by someone and I live in a state of apathy. I want and need attention. I suffer from constant automatic uncontrollable feelings of being worthless, hopeless and helpless. I feel extremely and uncontrollably sad, dull, dejected, very serious-looking, deeply disturbed and everyone avoids me. I don't like or want people to see me and I feel like running away/hiding. But it's also difficult to be alone because I am afraid and scared. I cannot stop feeling worthless and hopeless deep inside. I live in a state where I am full of constant and extreme fears (of being rejected, denied, being hurt, not wanted) and also feel betrayed and forsaken. I want to cry and weep deeply and madly but find it extremely difficult to start....

I am in constant pain and suffering, I have a very painful heavy head, feels like something big and large has been super compressed and forced into me, it feels seriously tight, stuffy and painful. I cannot stand the pain. The headaches very seriously hurt like I have a large injury inside. I am breathless and often feel out of breath, like there is not enough air. I also tend to hold my breath many a time, which can then lead to heavy breathing.

Concentration is another big complaint. I lack the ability to concentrate, reading is impossible and causes a lot of strain. It is difficult to watch TV or movies or listen to music. Poor concentration makes it extremely difficult and dangerous for me to ride/drive on the road in traffic. I am forgetful, I cannot remember things. When I am cooking my food, I tend to leave food boiling on the stove and forget. All of my vessels are black and stained at the bottom. I go to stores and forget what I had to buy.

I forget the list. At the ATM I cannot recollect my PIN. At home I cannot find things when I need them as I don't remember where I kept them.

My hands are unsteady and nervous; I cannot hold a pen steadily, my handwriting is poor (since childhood). My palms and feet sweat sometimes. Generally, my palms remain freezing cold. When I shake hands with people, they tend to withdraw instantly, saying it is freezing. This happens at the office every day. I have had a poor appetite since my childhood days and I often feel I lack a sense of taste.

Bharat also told me that he had severe throat pain that was aggravated by eating anything oily or if he ate or drank anything cold or chilled.

In this first case, the chief complaint is the experience of being worthless and hopeless. Translated into homeopathic language, this is indicative of the desperation the patient experiences in the given situation and this helps to identify the remedy.

As we can deduce from his report, the main story of the chief complaint is terror, fright and horror experienced to a degree of desperation and hopelessness.

DR ALI

When he had finished talking about his poetry, I asked Dr Ali to tell me about his main issues. He had come to me for his eczema, which he had since childhood, from his head to his feet. He even had itching and 'encrustation' inside his ears. The eczema on his face caused him embarrassment.

Dr Ali also recorded in his case form the main areas that were affected: under the knees, ankles, face and body, along with descriptive words 'prickling, bristling, itching, burning, dryness, something crawling on the skin'.

In another area, he described his complaint in detail, 'During severe attacks of eczema, sticky serum. Dripping wet. Smelly when exuding. Consistency is thin. On drying it looks like tiny amber crystals of sugar. Tolerably foul odour. Encrustation, contraction, drying exacerbates itchiness, restlessness, scaling, exfoliation.' He continued to say, 'The skin oozes so profusely, so much that people around would get up thinking that I am a leper and abandon me.'

In his case record form he recorded his main complaints and other associated troubles:

> Until the age of forty-three, I suffered from intermittent dermatitis on fingers, feet and toes. Homeopathy made my eczema a systemic disease. The change of seasons and places often induces an attack. I have also been getting recurrent bouts of sty in the eye for five to seven years. I also experience giddiness when sitting for a prolonged time.

In this case, the main focus of the chief complaint is that his eczema has made him look bad, disfigured and his appearance is very much affected.

CHETAN

Chetan came to me with Behçet's syndrome, which is an autoimmune disease associated with inflammation in various parts of the body. Recurrent ulcers in the mouth are a common symptom for this disease. There is no known cure for Behçet's syndrome in allopathic medicine.

He explained, 'Currently, I have ulcers on the tongue and in the scrotum area. The ulcers are itchy and there is a discharge from them.'

In his case record form he had written: 'The discharge is sticky, transparent, has an odour which is sweet like honey. The discharge is accompanied by a sharp, shooting and violent pain that comes and goes.'

He had also listed his other complaints: 'I have palpitations when lying in bed, especially on my left side. My sleep has been disturbed for the past two years due to my dreams. I never feel refreshed. I also get anxiety attacks and they developed after the ulcers on my tongue.'

In this case, the sharp, stinging and violent pains, which came and went very suddenly, were characteristic. Using his index finger, he would poke his palm repeatedly and aggressively to describe this stinging pain.

~

The narration of the chief complaint gives the homeopath a clue into the pattern of sensitivity in the patient. In the case of Bharat, his chief complaint can be seen as an expression of his pattern of terror and fright, and the sleeplessness, numbness and anxiety were a reaction to this.

In the case of Dr Ali, his complaints had to do with eruptions on the skin and the way he experienced these eruptions and eczema was as though he could not show his face to anyone. This was a reflection of a feeling of embarrassment, which is an expression of falling from one's position, and the feeling that one will be abandoned. This, we will discover, was reflected in all areas of his life.

In the case of Chetan, in his chief complaint was his experience of something stinging or poking him. There was the experience of something sharp and violent. We'll see in the coming chapters how this was central to the pattern of Chetan's inner experience.

We can see that in all three cases exploring the chief complaint offers vital clues of the inner pattern of an individual. The problem or chief complaint gives the homeopath a direction to see where the innermost pattern of the patient will lie. One way in which a homeopath can get a view of the inner pattern is to ask what is the main complaint or problem, be it physical, mental or emotional. There are two questions that must be asked: how does it feel and what effect does it have on the patient. The chief complaint of the patient is one of the clearest windows into his inner state. It is not the only window, however. In the next chapter we will see that the moment of crisis is another important window into who the person is.

8

MOMENT OF CRISIS

The moment of crisis is one in which an individual experiences the maximum amount of stress, or a situation that was most aggravating or exciting for him. Each of us have such moments in our lives. Usually, this can also be the starting point of some physical illness; for example, a huge grief, disappointment, anger, shock, someone's death, financial crisis, or a physical factor, such as injury, overexertion, etc. This crisis moment is also the point at which the features of one of the three kingdoms emerges very clearly and helps a homeopath decide whether a patient needs a mineral, animal or plant medicine.

Each person in his life has at least one or two moments of crisis. What the crisis is and how the person perceives it and reacts to it is a part of his unique individual pattern. One of the most important areas where the inner song of the person can be most clearly seen or heard is in a moment of crisis. In subsequent chapters we will see other such areas where the state is clearly visible and the person's compensatory mechanisms are least active, such as dreams, fears, childhood situations, behaviour, interests and hobbies.

It is at the moment of crisis that a person's real inner pattern or state comes out in an uncompensated and more direct form. Normally, most of us manage to create a comfort zone in accordance with our sensitivities. For example, if someone has a fear about being alone, he will ensure that he is surrounded by at least one other person at most times so he wouldn't experience his fear in everyday life.

In children, this state is much clearer and visible because compensation is minimal. Their fears, their grief, their sensitivities are much more openly expressed and can be observed accurately. Later on in life, a person tends to develop compensatory mechanisms to cover up these sensitivities. This is one of the key reasons homeopaths try to probe the person's nature and experiences as a child, that is, when his sensitivities were less hidden (see chapter 12).

A woman once came to me for treatment for an autoimmune disorder. The crisis factor was betrayal by her friend. This friend was a high-ranking politician who my patient had known for many years, and they had been very close. But when her friend attained a particular political position, she refused to do a favour that she had promised her. This sparked off my patient's problems. When I asked her to focus on that experience, she said she felt that the rug had been pulled from beneath her feet. She said it was as if the friend had suddenly turned into a monster and had shown a side of her which was hideous. As she focused on this sensation further, a more vivid image emerged. It was as if the friend had been hiding behind a mask, and when suddenly the mask came off, she saw a monstrous, deathly face. This gave us the clue to reptiles, which have a major theme of hiding. The remedy she needed was *Dendroaspis polylepis*, or black mamba, another snake remedy.

In a very recent case, I asked a patient what had been going on in her life just before she began suffering from her disease. She said that at that time she had known her husband, who was then her boyfriend, for one year, and she suddenly discovered that he was having a relationship with another woman. When I asked what her experience was at that moment, she said it was one of shock.

When I asked her 'What was your experience of that shock?' she said some very specific things. The shock for her had induced a physical experience of choking, trembling, getting palpitations and her feet feeling icy cold. These were very important symptoms—they were the characteristics for her remedy. Going further into this experience, she said that it was as if things were suddenly different. Things were unbelievable and new, and she wanted to cover herself, to shut herself up in her room with no light or noise, and to cling to something like a pillow, which would be her 'comfort zone'. And she said that she felt that all of her energy had been drained out of her, as if she could not even move her limbs. The remedy that helped her was *Nux moschata* which belongs to a plant group called *Magnoliales*. The specific sensation of this group is of being bewildered and confused, as if someone has been suddenly transferred to a strange, new and unfamiliar place. The consequent reaction is one of wanting to enclose oneself into a familiar sphere while shutting out the strange world.

Whatever has triggered someone's nervous sensitivity, emotional state or physical pathology provides a gateway into exploring the person's symptoms and experiences, which means the facts and the feelings that are most clearly representative of their inner pattern or state.

The crisis point of our three case studies were investigated and each individual's perception and reaction to the crisis is provided here to demonstrate clearly how each individual differs from others at a deeper level.

BHARAT

When we traced his childhood, Bharat mentioned having a recurring dream of his dead father. So, I asked him to tell me about his father's death. Bharat said, 'He died in an accident, three years ago or something. Frankly, I was glad he died. I had often wished that he had died a long time ago, maybe I wanted to kill him; there were so many times I wanted to kill him.'

This was definitely a sensitive issue I needed to know more about, so I asked him, 'Why did you want to kill him?'

Bharat answered, 'There was this incident that had happened a long time back—about eighteen years ago. He was hitting me, kicking me, thrashing me around. I ran upstairs and closed the door and he smashed through the door and he came in, and wouldn't stop kicking me for unknown reasons. After that I used to get continuous panic attacks. I couldn't sleep or eat. Another time, he slapped me on the face for no reason. I was stunned. I was frozen, my whole body went numb. I started to sob and I was so sad. A few days later, in the middle of the night I woke up and I was unable to breathe. It was like there was not enough air around. I was running around the house, so scared, I could not stand it. I was trembling and had palpitations. I was always terrified, scared and very afraid. I was afraid of life, I used to feel very vulnerable and sad.'

From his case record form, it was obvious that all of his troubles stemmed from childhood, and had to do with his father.

My father had always been a violent, impatient, self-centred and selfish individual. He seemed intent on hurting and overpowering me constantly for reasons I could never understand. As a child, at [the age of] four or five, I had severe sleep difficulty. I suffered from a lack of concentration and could not follow or understand anything. I suffered from a lack of energy and Dad would believe that I was lazy and would usually be angry. I was being sent to private tuitions, and to my misfortune, the lady there was a strict type who used a long, hard cane to communicate. I was often at the receiving end of this lady's anger. I struggled heavily to concentrate, learn and understand. I would often return home sobbing and crying bitterly. I could never follow what was being taught, I would be somewhere else mentally. I would also not remember what I was thinking or where I was mentally.

(I would fail constantly in tests/exams) and this would enrage Dad and he would never fail to show his anger and frustration at me. I had become non-communicative and very reserved. My sleep and appetite were bad and I always felt too tired to do anything. At this young age, I had started to have uncontrollable sadness and dull feelings. I was having a hard time trying to cope with nightmares and I had no one to talk to, not even my mom who was always reserved. As a kid, Dad kept denying me things. I remember wanting to play with a toy airplane very badly. I recollect begging him innumerable times to buy me one. But I was never able to play with one. We were a middle-class family and money was not an issue. In contrast, my elder brother and sister often got what they wanted, they always had plenty of nice clothes, but I had to be content with a few ordinary ones. Thus, I was constantly made to feel **unwanted and useless** by my father and this feeling is very, very strong even today. I recollect countless occasions of being badly abused and beaten up by Dad for the silliest of reasons.

From childhood through till adulthood, I have been a very quiet individual, actually too quiet. I would never speak to anyone, would always keep things to myself because I was **always scared and terrified**. Whenever there was someone visiting our home, I would actually run and hide in a room and not come out. I have never wanted anyone to see me. My father had always made me feel unimportant and worthless, and I grew up with this belief, and now today it's so deeply ingrained that I just cannot shake it off, it's become a part of me (part of my chemistry). I have tried to work with psychologists, medication classes, Reiki, etc. Nothing has had any effect except for *Nat Mur* (the only homeopathic remedy I have responded to), which has helped to an extent. But I continue to feel incessantly low, uncontrollably sad, terribly dull, worthless and useless.

I recollect three incidents from my past that completely devastated and completely undid me; the following is a brief description of them.

Incident (A): While I was in eighth standard (probably thirteen or fourteen years old), my mom had started to suspect my father of having an affair with the lady who lived in the house opposite from us. My siblings and I knew that there was nothing happening, but it was causing a great deal of disturbance at home. There was a long and a big fight later, and my father was seen slapping and kicking mom. It had crushed us kids to witness all this.

Incident (B): I was in tenth standard (sixteen years

old). Dad had just returned home from a business trip. He was in a foul and bad mood (probably a bad trip), and for an insignificant reason he slapped me on my head, just over my cheeks, with great force. I was sitting and eating dinner, and my plate was flung in the air. I had never been this shocked any time before. I sobbed endlessly for days and nights. It felt like I had been **permanently plunged into a dark, terrifying and unknown world**. A week later in the middle of night I had what I call a **panic attack**. I felt as though the electrical activity in my brain cells was interrupted. I was feeling horrible and had a great fear inside, my breathing was very hard. I felt as though I couldn't get enough air and was choking intensely. I also felt hot flashes, chills, chest pains, trembling, sweating, shaking very intensely. I felt a **terror** that was almost paralysing, along with the fear that I was going to go crazy or was about to die. I was running around the house jumping and banging on tables screaming 'I cannot stand this, please do something! Help me!' This lasted for quite some time until I became too restless and stopped. This episode had occurred suddenly, without any warning and without any way to stop it. The level of fear was way out of proportion. My brother called a doctor who lived in the neighbourhood at 2 a.m., who gave me an injection. And at his clinic the next day, he declared it was an allergic or acidic problem in my body without even inquiring what was going on in my life.

Incident (C): The incident above had hurt me very seriously, and even after a year I was suffering very deeply inside. Life was a mammoth struggle. I had unbearable and devastatingly sad and dull feelings that were consuming me. I had not recovered even in the slightest (I was actually deteriorating) and then it happened again, and the magnitude this time was several times higher and several times more damaging. My father trashed and smashed me, hit me around the house like a mad animal. I was being kicked, thrown around all over my house. This was my mad father at his worst, and his complete madness was on display here. My mom tried her best to come in the way to stop him and she was pushed away twice (she fell) by the mad animal that was my dad (my elder brother and sister were not at home). This incident spelt the end to my academics. I started to have panic attacks every day, I never could attend my college. I had literally lost my life, the damages done **inside me** were far beyond any words can ever describe. I was hospitalized for a fortnight at a large hospital in the psychiatry ward, and was put on a high dose of antidepressants following an attempt on my life. I would cry and weep incessantly, would constantly experience huge and severe palpitations, not eat anything for days, and would not sleep at all (I would be without sleep for several days). The above incident happened many years ago, but it's still fresh in me, like it happened recently.

Even now, thinking about it makes me lose control, choke and break down fully (I feel like breaking and smashing everything around).

DR ALI

From Dr Ali's case record form, it was revealed that he believed the origin of his illness to be 'Probably the trauma of losing my father early and swinging from prosperity to penury within less than a year. My orphanhood persists even now. I have not been able to outgrow this deprivation.'

He further revealed that his father died early in his life, and after that his family experienced poverty. This made him an outcast among his groups of friends.

CHETAN

Chetan explained to me when these symptoms started and it correlated with his crisis moment in life, 'These symptoms started when I was studying for my exams in college, and when I kept getting constant thoughts that my mother has breast cancer. Whenever I get these symptoms, I constantly move around, here and there. I have become very restless. I keep on moving around the house. I get anxious, and I feel I will lose my scrotum or my parts. I get worried and move here and there. I feel impulsive, hurried, and strange thoughts occur to me; like what will happen, will it turn into gangrene now? I am very quick in things, everything I do quickly, rapidly and impulsively. The thoughts come so quickly I have to take rapid measures. I keep on changing. I cannot stay with things for a longer time. Sometimes I get so depressed.'

Here, Chetan made an emphatic hand gesture by pounding his fist into his opposite palm: 'I keep hitting myself.' Again and again, he repeated this gesture and sentence. After a few moments, he said, 'I hate myself.' This time, he took his index finger and forcefully poked it into the palm of his other hand. Just like before, over and over, he repeated this sentence and gesture.

~

We can see that there is a difference in the three case studies with regard to the moment of crisis.

In the case of Bharat, the crisis moment was the brutal treatment by his father and when we understand this a little further, we see that this invoked in him fear and terror, which signifies his inner sensitivity and reactivity (features of the plant kingdom).

In the case of Dr Ali, we see that what affected him most was a loss. A loss of what he had (father, money, falling from a position). Losing his father at a young age induced the experience of losing something, pointing towards the mineral kingdom.

Finally, in the case of Chetan, we see that the crisis moment was anxiety regarding examinations and his mother's health and these invoked a somewhat complex set of reactions in which there were themes of 'I versus myself'. One versus the other, or one versus oneself, is a kind of competitiveness and aggressiveness, which points towards the animal kingdom.

So far, we have seen two windows which we can use to perceive the inner state: the chief complaint and the moment of crisis. These are still somewhat at a conscious level. There is one important window that is at a subconscious level, namely, dreams. Let us examine this in the next chapter.

9

DREAMS AND FEARS

One of the clearest windows into the subconscious and the pattern within each individual is his dreams, especially those that are very intense and repetitive.

The way a homeopath investigates dreams is unique. He does not interpret the dream at all, but rather, he takes the dream at the starting point of an exploratory process. He takes the patient into his/her experience in the situation of the dream.

The homeopath looks at the dream in two ways. One way is the facts of the dream itself—for example, dreams of the death of a relative, dreams of water or falling from high places. Dreams have been recorded in the testing and proving of remedies. A person's dream can indicate a specific remedy, and dreams are indexed in our repertories. The other way is to understand the experience of the dream; to let the patient narrate what his experience was in that dream situation.[1]

In both of these approaches to dreams, the one thing that is completely avoided is the interpretation of the dream. Several volumes in psychology have been written on the interpretation of dreams where the therapist interprets the dream of the patient. In homeopathy, however, it is believed there cannot be a standard interpretation of any dream whatsoever.

Each individual has his own experience of his dreams which ties in with his experience in all other areas of life, such as the chief complaint, moment of crisis, childhood nature, fears, etc. So we have to explore the dream to that depth, where the experience that has a common ground with experiences in all other areas can be discovered.

Slowly, a similar pattern emerges as with the first impression, chief complaint and crisis moment; the connecting thread of each one's individual pattern gradually comes into focus. By juxtaposing the narratives of the three patients this difference will become obvious.

BHARAT

When I asked about his dreams, Bharat told me,

> I would have dreams of animals, especially lions, chasing me. I would be terrified in the dream; so afraid. The other day, I had a dream where someone was trying to choke me to death. There are also times when wild animals attack me and it is very hard to escape. I get dreams of seeing a

lot of snakes in the well, and I am bitten by dogs. Animals attack and chase me. I get dreams of writing exams; I am scared and unprepared. I also had a dream of my brother being killed in an accident—his body was brought home. I was afraid to see his dead body, and I didn't want to see it. I was scared of the dead body. I was feeling so scared, and the image kept recurring.

When I was young, I dreamt that a ghastly bunch of lions were attacking my whole town. Everyone was running and many people were being killed. This was a long dream that dragged on.

DR ALI

In his case record form, Dr Ali listed many types of dreams which included travelling, trees, talking, sexual pleasure, nakedness, failures/exams, missing trains, and being unprepared for his examinations or lectures.

During the case taking, Dr Ali referred to a very clear, vivid and evocative dream, where he and his wife were engaging in sexual intercourse, when all of a sudden a child, of age nine or ten, appeared. She had sinister eyes and was just staring at me while I was performing; I felt fear as if she was a demonic creature or a witch about to cast a spell, but then she smiled at me and continued watching. She knew what was happening; maybe she would have threatened to blow the whistle to inform everyone of what I was doing.

For me, this dream was very interesting. So I decided to probe further and asked Dr Ali to tell me about this fear. He said, 'I have been uneasy about the act of sex. If you were to strip bare my psyche, you will find that there is an association of embarrassment, shame and guilt about the act. See how lewd and obscene it is. I won't be able to show my face. I should have guarded my privacy more.'

This dream led us down another fascinating path, when Dr Ali revealed to me, 'In the neutral sense of privacy, without breaching the sense of morality, you are entitled and free. In this sense, I like to move about in the house completely naked. I take precautions, like the curtains are drawn. I feel like one's skin should be allowed to breathe.'

I wanted to understand this deeper. He continued,

I feel completely at ease with myself. There is no shame even if I look myself in the mirror. I think it is okay. My wife pokes fun at me and says it is absurd, because I do this only when we are alone. She expects me to adhere to some norms, like a grandfather or something. This is like letting your hair down; like rolling in the dust without treading on somebody else; like wallowing in the mud like a buffalo. It is an experience of release and letting go.

This happens very often in the homeopathic case-taking process, where when we ask about something that is important to the patient, he narrates another incident, which is seemingly unconnected. However, at a deeper level, that incident is a reflection of the same inner experience.

I asked Dr Ali to explain this experience of letting go, and he narrated another story.

I was in this remote rural area about four years ago and I was conducting workshops and working in the offices, schools and churches there. Every day I would go for my morning walk. They had a beautiful full-sized bathroom in the hotel room, but when I would go for my walk, I would take my newspaper with me and defecate out in the open. I would enjoy defecating out in the open. I am that sort who would be striking a conversation with the other guy, a stranger who is metres away and shitting beside me. That kind of thing. The primitive people, their simplicity, the countryside and hills. I would fantasize there. In this place you feel unconfined and maybe you are as close to the earth as you will ever get as a civilized person. You suddenly know and make a quantum leap between the enlightened human being and the animal you know, which knows nothing, which has no sense or intelligence. At this level it is exhilaration. I feel very ebullient, very elated. I feel quite free and smooth. It is easy, I experience release. The way you empty your bowels, there is no straining, there is no discomfort except the niggling sense that you have to wash your hands somewhere with a cake of soap. It is like you are temporarily free from the golden cage of propriety and convention. That might cause the exhilaration. It is a solitary kind of desublimation that you come down from that altitude, that height, to a bottom level. And as appropriate, you can always re-climb to that altitude.

CHETAN

In the case record form Chetan circled a few types of dreams including travelling, sexual pleasures, illness, misfortunes, grief, failure and a day's work.

He had dreamt of a girl in his class whom he liked, and saw that she was pregnant by another man. In this dream, he experienced a 'heart-staking feeling'. This feeling was accompanied by the same gesture of him aggressively poking his index finger into the palm of his opposite hand. He felt so ashamed.

He spoke of dreams he had just a night before:

We were playing a final football match against the interns and I was feeling bad; I tried to get a goal, but it did not work. We lost 2-0. I was depressed; I was like hitting myself, biting myself because I could have gotten a goal. My friend betrayed me also, he teased me. He was my friend. If any other boy would have done this, I would not have minded; but because he did it to me, I was very upset. Betraying is like, you know, stabbing someone in the back with a knife. It is like cheating you without your knowledge and it should not have been done to you. It is a wrong behaviour, it is cheating.

He continued,

> Cheating means to fool you, it is to make you feel inferior about yourself. It is like looking down upon you. It is like beating you; it is better to beat someone than say things like this. I cannot tolerate cheating. It is better if someone hits me. It is like someone always takes things from you and you don't want to give it. It is destroying you! He is more superior than you are, you are inferior, nothing, zero, and he is the best!

During this whole dialogue, Chetan was emphatically moving his hands about, especially making the hand gesture of poking his index finger strongly into his palm. He was doing it quickly and aggressively.

~

Throughout the three patients' dreams, in the first case we see the terror coming up again and again. In the second case, we see that the patient is not embarrassed in a situation where normally it would cause embarrassment. Again, we see this embarrassment theme—right from the chief complaint, to the crisis moment, to the dream. In the third case, we see that there is a theme of competition with another man, aggressiveness, the same poking and stabbing gesture, and finally people doing things to him. Let us look at the dreams of our three patients in depth.

In Bharat's dreams, the inner experience is of being

pursued by something that is attacking him, along with the experience of fear, fright and terror, and a desire to escape. We can also see a degree of desperation and a kind of hopelessness. Compare this to the experience he had when his father was chasing him, wanting to beat him.

In the case of Dr Ali, we can see that even though he had several images in his dreams such as a child with sinister eyes, who was like a witch or demonic creature, the main experience of the dream for him is about shame and embarrassment, and the feeling of falling from his position as if his actions would be noticed and exposed. At the same time, there is the desire for his own identity and the choice to be himself. These are features that correspond to his inner experience, along with the chief complaint and other windows, namely loss and embarrassment.

In Chetan's case, we see here themes of jealousy, aggression towards himself, being deceived by another, comparisons leading to feelings of 'he is superior, I am inferior'. All of these themes form a pattern, which again points to the animal kingdom.

In short, without interpreting the dream, without theorizing about the dream, we attempt to find out what is the experience in the dream. Then we see that this experience ties in with the pattern we've already observed in the patient's conscious narrative. Dreams belong to the realm of the subconscious, but at a conscious level, we have other individualizing sensitivities to certain things. Closely allied to dreams are fears. Fears or phobias are specific for each individual and they offer a very clear window into each person's pattern.

Fears include what a person anticipates, his perceived fears, like fear of ill health, fear of being betrayed, fear of financial crisis, fear of his reputation being short-lived, fear of relationships getting spoiled, fear of death, fear of religious guilt or salvation.

As a homeopath, it is very important to ask what the person fears, anticipates, or what his worst nightmares are. Hope is on the other side of fear. Our specific hope represents the other side of what we fear. If our fear is of poverty, we always hope for wealth. If our fear is of loneliness we hope for a great relationship. What is the best-case scenario for a patient, for instance—is it rising to a position of power, just having a comfortable house, or travelling far and wide?

Both these extremes of fear and hope have very much to do with an individual's sensitivity and have to be explored thoroughly. When a person is afraid of disease, what does the disease mean to him? What will his experience of the disease be?

It is very important in homeopathy that we seek an answer not from logic or intellect but from a patient's experience. In the homeopathic process, when fears are talked about, logic has to be put aside. One has to ask for and receive information from a position of pure experience.

The patient has to be placed in the situation of fear, wherein a homeopath makes him go into that experience, and to actually relive it. If the patient attempts to rationalize his experience, he should be stopped. He must be repeatedly encouraged to experience in the moment.

Let us take a simple example: a patient has a fear of dogs. We ask him what he feels in the fear; he imagines that the dog will bite him. When asked to describe the experience, he may say, 'I will have to take anti-rabies injections, and I will be in so much pain. So much pain.' The deeper experience is the fear of pain. This will be seen throughout his life and childhood—even the momentary pain of an injection is perceived as something big.

Another person who has a fear of dogs might say, 'I imagine the dog is jumping at me, grabbing my throat and ripping the flesh apart. This horrifies me.' The remedy needed here is different from the one needed in the case above, proving that in the same fear or situation, different people can have different perceptions and reactions.

Similarly, if we talk about fear of poverty or loss in general, claustrophobia, fear of high or narrow places, each individual has a different experience of these. The homeopath needs to explore the deeper experience of these fears, in order to see that it has the same melody, frequency and idea as the experience in other areas of the patient's life.

In the previous chapters we have seen that what a patient experiences in his chief complaint, in his moment of crisis, in his dreams and fears represents his inner state. It is not only what a person experiences that is indicative of the pattern, but also what the patient does. One of the areas that we examine is interests and hobbies. It is this area where the person has a wider choice than his profession and he can choose to do what he enjoys. What the person enjoys has a lot to do with his inner pattern.

114

10

INTERESTS AND HOBBIES

A person's interests and hobbies, the things that he enjoys doing, and the things he needs to do compulsively are very important tools to understand his individual state or experience. Individual interests and hobbies are heavily influenced by one's individual pattern.

Often, many of these hobbies are actually symptoms in homeopathy. For example, singing, dancing, meditating, travelling, reading, theorizing, fantasizing, writing poetry and so forth are found in specific homeopathic remedies.

From the experience point of view, we need to find out what the experience of the individual is when pursuing these interests. What does it make him experience? It is, in fact, for that experience that he pursues this interest. Very often we can see that this experience is exactly opposite to the one he experiences in difficult moments such as moments of crisis, chief complaint, etc. In fact, quite often, the individual pursues his interests and hobbies as a kind of balance, to avoid that other unpleasant experience.

For instance, one patient told me that she 'enjoyed dancing a lot'. When asked about her experience of dancing she said, 'I feel free, unbound, released.' In the opposite situation, in her moment of crisis, she felt shackled, bound, constrained.

In another instance, there was a sixty-five-year-old man, who came seeking treatment for Lichen planus, a skin condition that can also affect the mouth and mucus membranes. It is an immune system disorder, and its treatment is ineffective in modern medicine. This condition is usually known to be caused by stress. The reason for stress in this man's life was his wife, who was suffering from a grave disease and was bedridden. She was paralysed; she could only move her head, she had complete paraplegia.

This experience was doing two things to him. The first thing was that he felt he was stuck in the house, always looking after her and nursing her. The second thing was that it caused him a lot of pain to see her suffer like that.

He told me that his passion was Indian classical music, about which he could speak at length. He would speak with a lot of excitement and his eyes would light up. He could find fault in the singers or pick up easily on the smallest nuances in the music. I almost thought he was a performer or singer himself, but he told me that was not the case and for him music was a diversion. It kept his mind away from the boredom and suffering in his house.

Sometimes a person's interest may be to help animals or to climb mountains. We have to understand what his experience is when he's doing that. These interests at times become a compulsion. The patient becomes more eager to seek them out, and for a homeopath, these experiences are very important. To illustrate this, I will narrate the stories of two professional tabla players.

I had a patient who was a very well-known tabla player. When I asked him what was his experience of playing the tabla, he explained that his mind would go into an ecstasy-like bliss. He would get lost and feel as though he were floating away in this blissful experience.

Then, I went to attend the concert of a vocalist who was accompanied by another well-known tabla player. What I saw here was totally different. This tabla player was extremely conscious of others watching him. He wanted to draw more attention to himself so he asked the volume of the tabla to be turned up on the soundboard, drowning the sound of the vocalists. His competitive nature could be seen clearly.

It is thus clear that an individual experiences the same thing differently from another. This information may not often be readily evident but by going into the experience of the individual when inquiring about his interest and hobbies, one can see it as the other polarity of his experience. This is also illustrated in the cases of our three patients.

BHARAT

Bharat's hobbies and interests included buying automobile magazines, to look at the pictures because he was fond of cars.

It was very difficult to get information from him, so I asked him what things on television and in movies did he not like. He said,

> I do not like to watch when someone is shouting or if someone is being abused or criticized. I do not go to see movies because I cannot control the volume or switch it off if I am scared. I am very scared when they show on television the shows about ghosts or when they talk about skeletons. I am very scared and have to turn it off.
>
> My interests and hobbies include downloading and watching English hit TV series, learning new ways to troubleshoot on MAC computers, and listening to music.

DR ALI

From the moment I received the case record form, I could see that Dr Ali was well read, intelligent and creative; he enjoyed writing poetry and had a knack for confusing me with his lyrical language.

He had published half a dozen short stories in well-known magazines around the world, and had even corrected mistakes in my case record form. Dr Ali also brought with him pages of his beautifully handwritten criticisms of my books and DVDs.

He also mentioned to me that he is 'not very gregarious, prefers solitude, desultory reading and to compose short stories and poetry. I am an avid radio listener, I owe 90 per cent of my education to many of the largest radio stations like BBC, VOA, Deutsche Welle and Radio Netherlands.'

He continued, 'Countryside walking tours, bird watching, tree spotting: I am an amateur naturalist.'

He was religious at one point in his life and would often write his own opinions, reinterpretations and critiques of excerpts from religious texts and scriptures. He had an interest in metaphysics, and in the search and quest for God.

CHETAN

I asked Chetan what things he liked to do, and he replied, 'I like playing football, talking to friends. There is a girl in my class; I like to spend time with her. I know there is no future for us, but still I cannot control myself.' At this point, Chetan made a large gesture with his hands, bringing them up into the air and moving them rapidly in a circle. He continued, 'Many a time she comes in my dreams also.'

Chetan did not watch movies. When I asked him which movies he liked he said, 'Movies, I don't watch those action movies and all. I like sad and romantic stories, classical stories, something which has a thought or which is very pleasant. I don't like too much noise. I get irritated by noise. I cannot bear loud noises at all. As soon as possible, I want to get away from the source or just switch off the source from where it is coming. I feel irritated and angry. It is very harsh; I get irritated, very irritated. I cannot control it. I hate watching movies that have fighting and are technical, with bikes and all. I hate movies with fighting or bombs. I don't like it when people fight each other and when they die. I hate watching when they kill [here, he pointed out something with a sharp edge in my office, picked it up and made a stabbing motion]. It's like to kill, with a knife or something, something sharp, something pointed. It is very cruel, very destructive and violent. I don't like it.'

I found this interesting, so I asked him to describe this further. 'It is like breaking things, you know, like killing people very cruelly, like in a gas chamber. They are burning, on fire, and then someone comes to shoot them with guns. I see people crying and I feel very bad.'

~

In Bharat's case, with regard to interests and hobbies, we can see that Bharat did not have any. This shows what an isolated life he lived. Also, it illuminates the reason he avoided any kind of entertainment, because with his sensitivity, he could not take the slightest amount of fear that could be aroused while watching a movie. He avoided all things that had the slightest possibility of generating fear, which tied in with the rest of his pattern. These attributes belong to the plant kingdom.

Dr Ali liked to do things that involved creativity, performance and language skills. He prided himself on these capabilities. To develop and to have ability and performance are qualities of the mineral kingdom.

In Chetan's case, he did not like to think of or see violence, killing, stabbing and cruelty—this was his sensitive spot. Such themes of violence, killing, one versus the other, and so on, are qualities of the animal kingdom.

In this chapter we saw the inner pattern of each person being reflected in what they do. In the following chapter, we will see how the inner pattern is reflected in how the person relates to others.

11

RELATIONSHIPS

Relationships can be the cause of maximum satisfaction or maximum stress and problems. In both cases, there are experiences that have to do with the nature and individuality of the person. The problems an individual faces in relationships as well as the significance they attribute to those relationships both have a lot to do with the inner pattern of the person. What kind of relationship the person seeks and what problems he has depend totally on his inner pattern.

Starting with a person's relationship with his parents, friends, spouse, children or associates at work, a homeopath needs to find out which relationships have the maximum stress or the maximum happiness associated with them and what the experience of each of these is. Even when in one of the relationships the individual is dependent on another, at a deeper level, the dependence can be of different types, like a child being dependent on his mother or like someone being dependent on his friend, or the dependence of a student on his guide. The homeopath has to understand the type of dependence. In a rare case, someone can even experience being dependent like he is a foetus in the womb of the mother, as the following case will illustrate.

I had a patient, a young woman with chronic sinusitis, who was in bed with her sinus problems almost all the time. She could not even leave the house. Her story was one of overdependence on her father and husband. She would call them on the telephone ten to fifteen times a day, and narrate to them every small detail of what was happening to her. Even though she was twenty-five years old, she would call her father and tell him details about her menstrual cycle.

Her biggest fear and nightmare was that she would lose her father or her husband, and this resulted in panic. When we probed into the experience, it was a feeling that if her father or husband were to die, she would lose her comfort zone. She described that comfort zone as 'something that enveloped her, something that surrounded her from all sides, and kept her totally out of contact with the world. It was a very warm, comfortable and undisturbed place.'

This almost exactly matched with what her sinusitis was doing to her—keeping her in the house, in bed, under the covers, and not allowing her to go out into the world. Her experience was similar to a foetus being inside the womb:

in a comfortable, enveloped and warm zone. After taking the remedy selected for her on this basis, not only did her sinusitis clear up, but her dependence on her father and husband, too, almost completely disappeared. She felt, in her own words, 'as if I have been born again'.

In another case, the relationship is one that affects the person's sensitivity all the time. Suppose you ask a patient how she relates to her husband, and she says, 'I feel constantly hurt by his words, which are rude, insulting and impolite. It feels like something sharp is poking me,' this is her experience of the relationship.

A third person could have a relationship where she feels constantly victimized. I had a patient who graphically described how much wrong her husband had done to her, how much he had tortured her, and how she felt so strongly that she wanted to actually tie him up, set him on fire and watch him suffer before his death. Fortunately for her husband, the homeopathic remedy helped her mental state and she developed some affectionate feelings for him.

We create our own stories, based on our perception or state. The homeopath attempts to find out what story the patient has created. What kind of relationship is he nurturing? With the remedy, this story can change because the perception changes.

The exploration of the nature of a person's relationship reveals the pattern of his inner experience and falls in line with the other aspects of his case. This is illustrated with our patients.

BHARAT

As we saw in the moment of crisis, for Bharat, the most important relationship dynamics were between himself and his abusive father, resulting in severe panic attacks.

I also asked about his mother and he said:

My mother, we hardly spoke to her. All she would do is cook in the morning and then most of the time she would lie down and that's all. Once, she suspected my dad was having an affair and it was a very bad scene. There was a big fight; dad was kicking, slapping and abusing her. We were all witnesses. At that time I was feeling very afraid.

As an individual she was always a very quiet, suppressed person who I feel was never really equipped to handle a husband and bear children and raise them (as I see it now). I do not recollect her showing me any love or affection and she has never asked me how I was after I came from school, tuitions or at any point while I was being raised. She would never be there when I needed a mother to talk to about my pains and my problems. Frankly, I despise her, and it would appear she has passed on a good lot of her problems through her genes to me. But I do appreciate the fact that she has not hurt me like my monstrous and evil father.

His father was dead and Bharat said that he wished his father had died much earlier. He also said that he wished that his father had never been born into this world or that he had died nine months before Bharat was born.

Describing his relationship with his elder brother, Bharat said:

When Incident-C happened, my brother was not at home and had he been there he would have definitely tried to restrain my father, and the extent/severity of damage which happened to me would perhaps have been lesser. He has been a fairly good brother and I am truly grateful and appreciative of that. But since the time he got married ten years ago he has become one of the most selfish individuals I know and he does not care for anyone else. After my father died, he has taken possession of some property and wants it to be his and would not allow it to be sold.

Of his sister, he said:

My father had a soft spot for her and she would get all that she wanted. I have a feeling that because he hated and despised my mother so badly, he had some love and feelings towards his daughter. During our childhood fights she would always get my father on her side and it would always be my fault. I recollect a horrid memory of my father smashing and beating me when all that I had done to her was nudge her for provoking me. She has never really been a balanced or a trustworthy person, and is temperamental. Her husband left her right after marriage when he learnt that he is married to a very rude, ignorant and disoriented woman. Personally,

I stay far away from this woman who happens to be my sister.

Of his associates at work: 'My serious and tense looks cause a huge problem; I learn that my fellow associates are at great discomfort. I have to work too hard to keep from being moved out of my job/company.'

I found out that he truly did not have friends. He said:

I do not have too many friends. When I go out with people I am quiet. It is like I cannot be in the middle of a conversation; I do not know what to say. Talking requires too much effort and is too tiring and exhausting, so I remain very quiet and also keep things to myself. I never attend or go to any get togethers, parties or weddings, etc. I tend to stay back home when colleagues go on outings/picnics. It feels odd to be with people, I just tend to not be with them. I would rather stay alone. I am greatly unhappy and saddened that I have never had a girlfriend. That I never go on dates. I am extremely jealous (although I don't show it) of colleagues and others who have girlfriends, feel crushed and saddened when I see couples having a good time in each other's company (it makes me feel lacking, reminds me of how disturbed and detached I am). If a girl looks at me I tend to feel extremely uneasy/unsteady and have to look away or escape. I have to avoid going to malls, parks, etc., or places where couples hang out or are on dates, as it brings about feelings of deep sadness, despair and apathy.

DR ALI

Dr Ali wrote in his case record form:

> I am something of a loner and I don't communicate much
> with the inmates of the house. Equations are cordial but
> my body language is that of a grave, angry, unsociable
> person. I do not like company much. I had quarrels with
> my mother a lot, she was naive and artless. I hated my dad.

He spoke about his children, 'My children feel I am very
reticent, and an absentee elsewhere in the world of books.'
One of his haikus that he wrote on the form was dedicated
to his first son having become independent, getting married,
and having a daughter. The second son was a bachelor and a
struggling actor. Dr Ali explained the meaning of the haiku,
'So, it is about the sort of slow drift between parents and
children as both of them are growing ideally in different
directions.'

He was a professor of English literature and had taught
for many years. He spoke about his time as a professor:

> The only reward, the only need I cherish in the evening
> of my life, is the unstinted appreciation (even adoration)
> from my students and peers that I am a good teacher, that
> my knowledge of English is sound. On the light side, I
> was repeatedly judged by the crème de la crème as the
> cutest, coolest and the friendliest professor in the faculty.
> I think this gives you gratification which you cannot get

through the acclamations like a trophy or a scroll, or a souvenir, or a certificate.

Dr Ali addressed his wife a few times in the case, whom he spoke of when talking about his dreams. He continued to tell me stories about his wife, including one story at the dinner table: she told him to eat whatever was kept before him, and he simply responded to her, 'Maybe I am elsewhere.'

I felt this was strange, so then I asked him, 'Then where are you?' He responded:

> I am usually either anticipating something or remembering something, but I am sort of temporarily abstracted from the present. Sometimes I ask my wife how many chapattis I have had and she says that it is an idiotic question. Sometimes I remember stanzas, poems, which I maybe memorized fifty-five years ago. I wouldn't forget them; some elegancies of Shakespeare or some dialogues from plays and dramas.

Dr Ali liked to theorize in his mind and was himself an intellectual. He mentioned that he also enjoyed interacting with the 'riff-raff, ragpickers, tramps, roadside vendors, manual workers and beggars'.

CHETAN

Chetan mentioned in his case record form a variety of relationships. He wrote: 'I like company very much and enjoy being with college friends. I am jealous of my friends who are rich and healthy.' During the case taking Chetan explained, 'What bothers me most is when I lose a match to friends who are not as good as I am. I feel like hitting them, but then they are my friends and I cannot hit them.'

He explained his nature further:

I get irritated fast. I get very angry, angry at friends who try to outsmart me. I also get angry if someone tries to win over me. I cannot do anything and feel hopeless. I feel like breaking things or hitting things. Hitting my head on things. I want to break things very fast, like a pencil. I want to hit [here, he made repeated gestures of hitting his fist into his palm]. Hitting a wall, or the bed, even myself sometimes.

I don't like it when people tell me about my drawbacks. It also makes me more sensitive. I try to control my bad habits like lying. I feel like I should be a better person and feel guilty. Guilt comes and then I start losing games.

In addition to this, he wrote of how he liked a girl in his class and knew there was no future for their relationship, but he couldn't rein in his feelings for her. 'I am disturbed about her because I like her. I dream of her but it does not affect my studies. It is just that I like to spend time with her. I have uncontrollable feelings for her.'

He explained that his greatest disappointment was not winning an election in his college. He was running for the position of general secretary of the student council. In the case record form he wrote:

> I am the cultural secretary, so I think if something should happen it should be the best, like very creative and perfect. I try my best to achieve and show that I am good, that I am the best at something. It is important to be ahead of others and before they [can] think, because I want everyone to know about me and appreciate me. Perfect means the best—it is good, good-looking, attractive, something which is good for people to look at. Even if I draw something it should be the best drawing with the perfect shades.

Chetan continued to explain:

> Most of the time I am in college. I spent very little time with my parents. Moreover, they are busy with their life. When I go home they are watching TV and I do my studies. I do not like to spend a lot of money. Thus, I don't go out with my friends to watch movies. I do not have a mobile phone also. I just like to travel with my friends. I get irritated at my parents when they keep asking me about what I am doing. I tell my sister when something is wrong or if I want some money, otherwise my parents don't talk to me a lot. Most of the time, they are busy watching TV and it hurts me. They do not understand me. I feel alone and do not talk to them, it's like I am unlucky or something. It is something which I am not getting, but

131

it is not mine. It is something that is constantly poking [hand gesture of poking index finger into palm]. It is continuously hammering, poking, pricking and constantly hurting. It is sharp and stitching. Sometimes I feel bored and alone, and then I get angry and irritated. Sometimes I even break things and get violent. I have injured myself as well. I feel like just beating up something.

He told me about an incident with his father:

When I was not selected for the election of general secretary of the college, my father said, 'What, you cannot do this also?' So I started crying and felt he was teasing me, I felt so inferior. Like a beggar, like a poor person, like no one. It is like you know nothing; you are like a no one. The opposite is to be the best and to be number one. I wanted to be the head of the council. I would be so happy if I was the boss. I would feel very proud and do the things the way I wanted. I could order whomever I wanted. Everyone would follow what I said. For me, being the boss is being on top and everyone following my orders.

~

A relationship which is aggravating or which is good can point towards the state, the reactions, the individuality and experience of the person. In each person, the state of individuality is what sets up these relationships in the first place. It is our state and our perception, our sensitivity and our aggression that invites these relationships around us or influences the way we relate to people. It is not who they are, but what we perceive them to be, or what we perceive them doing to us, that is actually more important.

In the case of Bharat, from the nature of his relationships we see the experience is again of fear, a feeling of isolation, abandonment and terror. This ties in with his earlier history.

Dr Ali relates to people by performing and seeking appreciation for his talent and skills. This means he is seeking value for what he has. As far as Chetan is concerned, he relates to people by competing with them, trying to be superior to them. In understanding a person's relationships and the problems that arise, we get another glimpse into his inner pattern, but often this aspect is something that he has thought about and therefore, his experience is coloured by his thoughts and theories about what is happening. A purer picture of his inner state and pattern is available to us at a time when his thoughts and theories were not so developed, namely, his childhood.

12

CHILDHOOD

In childhood, a person's state is in its most clear, undisguised form. As we grow into adulthood, we acquire compensatory mechanisms for our feelings and fears. For example, if someone has a fear of being attacked, he might take lessons in martial arts, so that this fear is somewhat alleviated. We also tend to rationalize things, in order to not feel disappointed or hurt. However, in a child, where such compensatory mechanisms and rationalizations are not in place, the feelings and fears are seen more clearly.

Since a person's state, to a large measure, is one that starts from his conception and ends with his death, any information from any period of time in his life is a part of that state. While in a majority of patients the inner pattern remains more or less constant for a considerable period of their lives, in some patients this can change, and another song from a different kingdom can become more dominant.

It is better to not classify and fix a patient permanently in a specific kingdom, but to closely examine what his experience, perception and reaction is at that given moment in his life and then find the remedy from the appropriate kingdom.

Just as we found the chief complaint, moment of crisis and dreams among the clearest expressions of the person's state, similarly, an exploration of the person's nature, state and incidents that happened in his childhood, are a very important part of this inquiry.

What is important to note, unlike Freudian theories, is that the homeopath does not subscribe to the view that adult pathology or psychopathology is the effect or result of childhood incidences or trauma.

The idea of cause and effect is somewhat alien to the homeopathic thought process. In fact, homeopathy takes an exactly contrary viewpoint. The homeopath sees phenomena as it is and does not ascribe a cause to it because he believes the idea of causation is a theory at best. The truth is the experience of the individual, rather than why it is, or what caused it, which is a theory.

By understanding the experience of an individual in a given situation, one can see that the same experience pervades all the situations in a person's life and, therefore, the idea of causation recedes further.

What we see is that in the same situation, even in childhood, two individuals perceive and react to that situation in a completely different and individual manner. To ascribe a person's state to a certain incident or cause is not logical. What the homeopath attempts to trace is the commonality of the experience in various situations; the experience, reaction, and behaviour in childhood become an important link in the chain.

For instance, I have a patient who is currently being treated for hypertension. He always brings his wife to the consultation and she does all the talking. The patient is often quiet and simply nods in agreement with whatever the wife says. If I ask him a question, he hesitates with his reply and the wife takes over. From this I understood that this patient is heavily dependent on his wife, has low self-confidence, is not able to easily face situations and people, and is unable to take decisions. When I asked about his nature as a child, I saw the confirmation of this pattern: he was very shy, introverted, had no friends, had always felt incapable and inferior, and was an object of ridicule.

When he was a child, if he saw his friends talking and laughing about something, he imagined they were talking about him and making fun of him. As a child, he was very irresolute, and even simple decisions such as what to wear or eat would need external intervention. He is presently the manager of a bank and has a good position. To the outside world he does appear confident but our subtle observation of his behaviour, along with the clear picture of his state as a child, gives us a very good insight that he himself feels deficient and inferior. This is the picture of the remedy *Baryta carbonica* (see also chapter 5).[1] This medicine helped this patient in both areas of his life, physically and emotionally.

When exploring various cases, we see that the reactions of a person in childhood are also very individual. Bharat's, Dr Ali's and Chetan's cases illustrate this.

BHARAT

This is from a family photograph of Bharat's, when he was a child. Note the apprehension and fear in his eyes.

Bharat explained his childhood and his nature as a child:

A tense, scary childhood. My mother was very quiet and non-interactive. She was buried, lost in her own issues. Dad was the reserved, strict type. I was a vulnerable, lonely type. I used to be very, very scared. Especially of my dad. He was a scolding type and I couldn't handle his scoldings, his arrogant behaviour and beatings. I once tried to hit him back with the same stick he used on me at five or six years of age to show how much he hurt me, and he grabbed the stick and beat me on my back with it. It was horrific. I wept and wept all by myself. I kept sinking into a deep, dark, sad world. I have been depressed deeply since as long as I can remember. I have lived and survived on fantasy dreams, started masturbating very young by pressing my genitals hard.

The incidents mentioned in chapters 7 and 8 occurred during Bharat's childhood and he said they completely devastated him.

DR ALI

As noted earlier, in chapter 8, Dr Ali lost his father at a very young age. He also lost his brother to suicide. Dr Ali recorded in his case record form, 'I had an excessive dependence on Mom. I thought Dad didn't love me. I was a touch-deprived child. Touch shyness, this persists even now. I lost my father when I was eight or nine. Abject penury and orphanhood exacerbated my inferiority complex and rendered me tongue-tied.'

In one of his poems, Dr Ali says, 'Was brought up on scraps and crumbs from relatives. I have hated the indignity of dependence, parasitism all my life.'

He recalled during the case taking:

When I was a kid, my mother would come to my bed at night and she used to say, 'Oh, God! Give me understanding, give me health!' This was her iconic saying. She also said, 'Your mind will open and then you can go ahead, you will see knowledge and light.' When I was preparing for one of the biggest examinations in my life, my mother used to worry and used to tell me at 3 a.m. to go to sleep. My mother told me that people who studied too much went mad. So my mother never asked me to study, she always requested me not to study. She would even tell me, 'Look you are reading while you are eating!' She explained to me that I never knew what food I ate and I never even asked for food. I only wanted to study.

He continued:

As a child, I was irritable, shy, inhibited, frail, emaciated but not sickly. I was lonely, pugnacious. My father ignored me. I was father-deprived, possessive of my mother, violent and obstinate. I was punished by my father violently. I used to beat and stone innocent animals and beat my younger sibling, my brother. He was schizophrenia-prone, frail, and committed suicide in 1988.'

In his case record form, Dr Ali wrote a note: 'Important: Precociously aware of sexuality. Was attracted to the opposite sex when I was six or seven. I knew about the birds and the bees much before my peers did.' At age seven or eight, he was 'infatuated with a girl, which was one-sided. Early experiments with masturbation.'

In his case record form, the qualities in his childhood

which he ticked included obstinacy, disobedience, rebelliousness, aggression, hyperactivity, destructiveness, courage, stealing, telling lies, shyness (here he had put two tick marks and written 'too much'), unusual attachment to his mother, a desire to hurt animals and humans.

He also said that he 'was a nocturnal creature for over a quarter century, who loved loafing around, studying and listening to music throughout the night'. He was at the top of the class in school and was proficient in five languages by the time he reached graduation.

CHETAN

Chetan is a twenty-one-year-old, so he is basically still in his younger years. However, he recalled one story of his childhood that was very significant.

There is one situation that deeply upset me. Whenever I refuse someone, someone who comes to me and asks me for something, then I refuse and keep on thinking about it afterwards. This time a girl had come and asked me to lend a cricket bat. It was my best cricket bat, and she was begging me to lend it to her. I did not want anyone playing with my bat so I refused! I had a fear of losing it, thinking someone will break it. So, I did not give it to her, but then I felt very bad because I feel that God gives you things that you can give to others, but I did not give my bat to her. I couldn't play also; I started losing all the games after this. I felt like I had made a big, grave mistake. I felt very bad and useless. I felt ashamed, like I couldn't even do this much. Ashamed is like being greedy and not giving things to others, like there is no self-respect. It is like not having control over yourself.

Physically, Chetan had taken an allopathic drug for allergies and got a rash as a result. He had small spots, similar to pimples. He also had ringworm in the thigh region and groin, for which he was taking antifungal medication.

In his case record form he ticked the qualities he had: hyperactivity, destructiveness, competition and winning spirit, sibling jealousy, boasting, stealing, telling lies, biting nails, religious, laziness and indolence. He ticked sensitive and emotional too. He mentions in his case record form, 'I lie a lot. I cannot control it. I try not to lie but I lie a lot to my friends and family to prove myself right.'

Chetan also explained that, 'For a long time (since childhood) I cannot read for a long time because after a few minutes I will have to change what I am doing.'

~

In Bharat's case, there is an emphasis on the relationship with his father, which instilled an experience of fear and terror during his childhood, leading to his reaction of hopelessness and despair. Again, we see the confirmation of the same inner experience coming up in many areas of his case.

Dr Ali emphasized the desire for achievement, to read all the time, and to be intellectually sound right from his childhood until the present moment. All of these facets have to do with his personal capability and skill and the desire not to lose them—a mineral kingdom feature.

In Chetan's case, you see that there is a conflict—should I give her the cricket bat or should I not give her the cricket bat, in addition to hyperactivity, destructiveness and competition. This conflict, representative of the 'I versus me' theme has been seen repeatedly in his case.

How the person was in his childhood reveals his pattern, but also how a person lives his life at present can be a good indicator of his inner state. That is why a homeopath also looks into the lifestyle of the patient.

13

LIFESTYLE

The inner state colours everything, but where it is very obviously seen is in the difference of lifestyles. What is the occupation that a person chooses? More importantly than the occupation itself, how does he view the occupation?

A medical doctor came to me with a severe allergy in his entire body. His throat would get constricted and he would need to be admitted to intensive care in order to save his life. After a few such episodes, he came to seek homeopathic help. I saw that he was a medical doctor, so I asked him what he was doing as an occupation, and he said, 'I am doing business.'

I thought it strange because he had a medical degree. He said, 'Business is money. I work the whole day and night.' As his story went on, I found that in his desire for business and money, he neglected his wife and child. He just talked about his dreams of doing business and making money.

He had told me that once he had gone to Agra. I asked him how the Taj Mahal was, and he said he never saw it! He was there only for business. 'The Taj Mahal wasn't for sale, and so I did not bother to even see it.'

He continued to say, 'Money earns respect and position.' So, after hearing this, I tried to challenge him and asked, 'What if India's richest man was walking on the street, and on the other side of the street was Mother Teresa. Where would there be more followers?' He grudgingly admitted the crowds would be with Mother Teresa, but just as I thought I had stumped him he continued, 'It is only because she has so much money, and that money helped her so she could build so many institutions. Just imagine, if she were a simple nun, working in a remote slum in Calcutta, would anyone know of her or respect her?'

By the time he was done, I myself was nearly convinced that business and money were the most important things. The remedy that helped him was *Bryonia*,[1] whose main symptom is 'thinks, talks, and dreams of business'.

There was once a woman who had multiple sclerosis, who was an accountant at a bank. One would think this is not a very important position, but when I asked her about her job, she said, 'I had the key to the office, and without me, the day wouldn't start. I was the most responsible person.' She was only an accountant, and yet she saw herself at the most important position in her workplace, with this responsibility. From childhood, she had this independence and sense of responsibility in her. She received the remedy

Plumbum metallicum, which helped her tremendously with her symptoms of multiple sclerosis.[2]

How people pursue their vocation is very individual to them. For instance, one homeopath can see himself in a creative role, doing research. Another can see herself in a political role, creating a voice for homeopathy in the world. One may just be a routine homeopath, who treats patients daily, in and out. Another may be a showman—he wants to be in the news and on television. The way people dress is also a result of how they perceive themselves.

In this area, the observations of the patient's relatives and friends are also interesting. These people can describe to the homeopath what they perceive of the nature or temperament of the patient: irritable, anxious, angry, silent, shy, decisive, indecisive, responsible or irresponsible. Furthermore, they can describe the typical behaviour of the patient. The simplest example is an observation that someone is extremely fastidious and particular about how things are kept.

One patient told me that he had his fourth-standard report card still preserved, even though he was seventy-five years old—this kind of detail.

One woman may be overanxious if someone in her family is not home on time, calls them several times, cannot sleep, pacing back and forth until they are home, and is always anticipating something might have gone wrong.

These traits of a person's nature, lifestyle and occupation are vital clues. These are things that the person usually cannot help doing or being because of his own inner state. The way the person lives his life, his occupation, his nature and temperament, his social circle, his dressing style, his position in his family and society—all of these are often heavily influenced by his inner state.

BHARAT

As described in chapter 5, Bharat was wearing a woollen sweater and appeared terrified and meek as he had just entered the clinic after an altercation with a taxi driver. He worked at a call centre and had completed his schooling following the experience in hospital (see chapter 12).

Bharat explained in his case record form:

Work, both mental and physical, is difficult and almost impossible. Getting myself to work and the office is a huge task and I am most often late. It pains all over my body without physical reason. Always restless as I cannot get enough sleep. . . .

I feel extremely sensitive like I live on the edge just about balancing my life and the slightest contempt or provocation from outside is impossible to bear, and I feel great discomfort and irritation. I find it almost impossible to mix with people and say, have a conversation. I tend to get very hurt when someone speaks roughly or is expressing some anger, sad feelings, or frustration. It is impossible to stand/hear someone crying, even a baby. I have to close my ears or run. I am extremely irritable and vulnerable. It is impossible to hear/bear anyone talking about sad things, and things like ghosts leave me completely frightened and terrorized, and it can take days even to get some composure back. I feel I should not have any sharp objects in my sight—knife, blade, sharp scissors, and even pen tips. I would use them to hurt myself.

DR ALI

As we know, from earlier chapters, Dr Ali was a professor of English, master of many languages, and was revered by his students. In his case record form, he recorded additional remarks:

1. I am a man of slender means and very, very few wants.
2. Consider animals, trees, and birds my brothers and sisters.
3. Spend most of my time alone with a book. A bibliophile. I am fond of music, nature and writing.
4. I am profoundly spiritual in a non-institutional way.
5. Very irascible and prone to a melancholy and agnostic outlook.

He also recorded that he was a 'Great dreamer and day dreamer'. He wrote spontaneous words very randomly throughout his form, like eccentricity, fantasy, creativity, exemplary felicity with words and pronunciation, intonation; handwriting, creativity, patience, fortitude, improving with age.

Dr Ali quite proudly informed me, 'I am simple and spare. It is a voluntary asceticism. I have been wearing used clothes bought from pavement vendors. I wear rags. I don't care what anyone thinks of me. I will lead my own life.' In his case record form, he wrote in the margins, 'For more than half my life I have been wearing used clothes. I get a high which an Armani or Yves Saint Laurent cannot give me.'

For Dr Ali, his privacy was extremely important:

Personal privacy, like my privacy, is everything which is unacceptable by outsiders, by people, by preachers, by believers. Like, in my heart of hearts, I question God. So this is privacy to sort of ventilate these ideas in my poems or short stories. In a very, very symbolic form, why these people prosecute you, your family, those who are related to you, they become the victims. There is an awful lot of barbarism, which is caused by knowledge. I mean the normal way would be saying that people are blinded by ignorance. I think there is something worse than that and that is people being blinded by their knowledge. Their knowledge of God, their knowledge of religion, their knowledge of ethnicity that is worse, that kind of thing. Ignorance, at least you can redeem the people who are ignorant, but those who are blinded by knowledge, my God! Private space would subsume all those things which are supposed to be sacrilegious, immoral and disrespectful. You allow these thoughts to visit yourself sometimes, you mutter over them under the breath, but you would not if your wife was around, if your son was around, your daughter was around. You would not be able to utter those imprecations or those thoughts because they would misconstrue you that you are at the evening of your life, decaying and maybe you need to see a counsellor.

I was interested in this 'evening of his life and decaying', so I asked Dr Ali to elaborate:

Retirement. I mean, not in the sense that if I were to approach someone for some assignment, chances are that nine out of ten people are impressed by my knowledge or skills, but then eventually they say, 'Look, you are a retired person and we wish we had someone less old.' One feels a little hurt because it is an ageist kind of society. That people judge you on the basis of your years. This comes from the occident—over in the West. If you are over forty years there, they reject you, saying that you are overboard, that you are just flotsam and jetsam. I don't feel bad now as much as soon after I retired. Like, for example, someone was to underpay you, like instead of 5000 he will give 2000. I will say OK, don't give me 5000 but give 4000, you can discount for my ageing or because I am a geriatric. My output may not be as buoyant or as sound as that of a young man.

CHETAN

From the first time I saw Chetan in that debate (see chapter 5), I began to learn about his nature. As a student in college he had a good presence and attracted much attention through his behaviour; obviously, he was creative and talented in speaking and overall, very popular among his peers.

We also saw more of his nature in chapter 11—jealousy, a tendency to lie and steal, impatient, hurried, impulsive, restless, irritated, uncontrollable sexual-related feelings, boasting, and finally, his desire to be the best and on the top.

I probed about his restlessness and impulsiveness. Chetan said, 'I always want something. I always want to do something that people appreciate. I always try to answer and am working hard for that [hand gestures of index finger pointing to palm], I want to get the details that people do not know. I want to know what others do not.'

He explained a little about his nature, his hands moving about rapidly. I asked him then about this gesture of poking his palm quickly and aggressively. As it often happens during case taking, Chetan did not respond directly but said instead:

I want to get things very fast. This is my habit from the beginning to answer in the class. I like to give quick answers, and before everyone answers I like to give the answer. You have to be very quick and you should know each and every detail, the small, minute details—I am very quick to answer. Then I get praise and appreciation. Many times I do this so others notice. They appreciate that I answer so quick, very quick. I want to be ahead of others, on the top or peak of the mountain, superior. Like you are known for that and no one else can have it. I want to be superior, the best. And if I don't give those answers I feel very depressed. I feel very bad. It is like being ashamed, like how can I not answer this? It's like defeat, you know. The opposite of being on top is to be common, to be mediocre, and to be with everyone on the same level. It is very low. Like everyone is low. This is bad. You are like everyone, on the same level.

It is like when I lose a match, a football match or a table tennis match, I feel very bad. I feel like there should be this rewind you know; again I should get the thing to answer it or to play the match again so that I could win it or something like that.

Here, Chetan made a rapid gesture of his hands rolling over one another.

~

Bharat lived a very isolated life, in which he felt terrorized and frightened by everything, including ghosts; he was a very sensitive individual. Again, this reflects what we have already seen about him in terms of his fear and terror, as well as his feelings of isolation. We can see how the pattern reflects in his lifestyle.

In the case of Dr Ali, there is an important realization: he is in the evening of his life where he feels he is decaying. The elements of embarrassment and privacy also come in here. Through Dr Ali's lifestyle, we see again the inner pattern of loss and losing his position, resembling the themes of the mineral kingdom.

In the case of Chetan we again see his competitive nature, wanting to answer first and fast in the classroom situation, and the general feeling of being defeated by another. The themes of competitiveness, aggression and the desire to be superior, in his lifestyle as well, again indicate the animal kingdom.

14

ADVANCED TECHNIQUES

With the shift in homeopathy from a purely factual and symptom-based level to a more subtle experience or sensation level, there was a further need to create and develop advanced techniques that could help access the experience or sensation level.

As homeopaths, we had to aim to find avenues by which the patient's sensation could speak directly to us, without the filter of the logical mind, which often tries to classify and interpret the experience, rather than just allowing the experience to be. These advanced techniques include using the imagination, the meditative experience, doodles and a conversational approach.

Using the Imagination

One way of accessing the patient's core experience is through the imagination. A technique that I am trying out

153

in this direction is to give the patient one word, ask him to picture it and list five words that come spontaneously to him.

One of the words that we use in this technique is 'wall'. I first ask the person to imagine a wall, any wall. They should then write down five words that spontaneously come to mind when they picture a wall. I then ask the person to read out the words; out of these, two or three words may describe the wall in some way. The other words are likely to be more subjective.

One patient mentioned these words: brick, paint, tall, strong, protective. I asked the person to take only the subjective words like tall, strong and protective. I then suggested that these words form a pattern. I asked the patient to forget the wall and to focus on the pattern formed by these words and to narrate the experience.

In this case, the patient mentioned that when focusing on the pattern formed by the words tall, strong and protective, she experiences the sensations 'safe, comfortable, circumference, protected, relax and cosy'.

The homeopath can ask the person to go deeper into this experience and see what emerges. We can also ask the person to provide the exact opposite of this experience. Here, the person mentioned that the opposite experience was of 'incomplete, open and exposed'.

Through this experience and its opposite, one can get a fairly good idea of the core experience of the person and this can be used to confirm the remedy.

Meditative Experience

Parts of the homeopathic process find parallels in Vipassana meditation. Vipassana is a way of self-transformation through self-observation. It focuses on the deep interconnection between mind and body, which can be experienced directly by disciplined attention to one's physical sensations.

I would like to describe the meditative experience that I sometimes use as an approach in case taking. I am cautious about borrowing approaches derived from other disciplines in my homeopathic practice because I believe that these disciplines, as practices in their own right, require theoretical training, practical knowledge and supervised guidance. Yet when used carefully and appropriately, a meditative approach can be highly effective in allowing the patient to go into the deep levels of case taking, from which he can most effectively communicate his core experience.

In some cases, if we observe that the patient is ready and that there is no risk involved, we can suggest that rather than thinking about it, the patient go into the experience and live it in that particular moment. In this way he can bring the experience to his consciousness and then become a witness without any thinking or judgement. This experience of the patient can be a part of or the whole of his core experience.

It is important to understand that in this process we do not use any special techniques. Closing the eyes is often automatic for the person and does not usually require direct instruction because when fully focusing on an inner experience, the view of one's physical environment is distracting.

The aim of using the meditative technique is to make the patient more aware of his experience. When a person is describing his anxiety, it is clear that he is not only narrating, but also beginning to experience the anxiety in that moment. For me, this is the entry point for use of this technique. I can then tell him, 'Focus all your attention on this anxiety.' After some moments, in which he connects with this state, I can ask him what the experience of the anxiety is.

We can also use entry points such as strong memories of a crisis situation, or a vivid sensation of physical pain occurring in the main complaint of the person. You ask the person to start experiencing that in the present by relaxing and directing all his attention to it. The homeopath has to create an atmosphere in which there is ample space and time, with no distractions, and has to fully trust that the experience of the person will reveal itself in the process, whatever comes up.

It is important to gently encourage and reassure the person. This gives him the confidence and sense of safety to allow the experience to deepen. Questions must be gentle and non-leading, and the homeopath needs to be completely open to whatever comes up. The patient must never be pushed or prodded.

If, despite gentle assurance, the patient is simply unable to go forward with this process, then the homeopath has to stop. However, generally speaking, if you have begun the process with someone who has shown that they are ready for such an experience, you simply need the patience to allow plenty of time and space for it to go forward.

Out of the three case studies, only Chetan was able to go into a meditative state. In fact, his ability to go into a meditative state along with his doodles allowed me to find his medicine effectively.

CHETAN

Watching Chetan wave his hands in the air and use his index finger to poke forcefully into his palm continuously became very interesting for me. Somehow, the energy of this case was in this restlessness and the motion of the hands. So I told him to close his eyes and stay with the rapid action of his hands.

Over the next half an hour, Chetan went into a meditative state. The following excerpts of the case transcript describe Chetan's meditative journey:

D: Just stay with this gesture. Close your eyes, just stay with this action. Do it again and again.

C: [Hitting his palm with the index finger of the other hand] Something which I am not able to control. Hate or jealousy. I want to hit myself.

D: Forget yourself. Totally forget everything you said. Just focus on this movement and this action. And whatever comes, you tell me.

C: [Repeating the gesture] This red thing is coming in front of me, and there is a mountain. I can see an eye, which is closed.

D: Just concentrate on these images and go with them. A red thing . . . a mountain . . . an eye, go with it and see what else comes.

C: More redness. A bird. Again a closed eye. There is something hot there. Vapours coming out of the pot. And a lot of water in it. Arrows are coming out. Again a closed eye and a red spot. Something which is very bright. It's black. There is a bright spot. Everything black.

D: Go into the black and the bright spot and see what happens.

C: Bird . . . A snake, he is eating the bright thing, the snake is eating the bright thing. He ate it. A flower, a lotus flower. Flower is moving round and round, again a snake. [Thrusting his fist into his palm] This flower. This shell, this shell. [Repeats the above gesture.]

D: What happened? What did you experience in this movement?

C: I am slipping down and a black thing was there. There is this mountain. Big mountain, a red well, and an insect coming to me. An insect is coming towards me. It's something like a scorpion, a small bug. It's moving towards me. They are many . . . I am going through them . . . there are many, many insects ... I am going through them ... big spiders too ... [moving both hands as if wading].

They are all dead now . . . there is this red water . . . now they are all dead. There is a well and it has a [tall] tree going up to the sky. Its long leaves are growing, growing to the sky now with a lotus flower on the top and with thorns on it. I am going up, up, I am climbing the tree. I can see birds flying in one direction and there is a bright sun. The sun is moving very fast and there is a temple. A long road, very long road, it's going up the mountain. The temple is on top of the mountain and I see the red thing falling from the temple . . . the red thing is going down . . . this round, red thing . . . down . . . down . . . down . . . going down. Down . . . going down . . . going down . . . down.

D: What did you see?

C: Going down. Going down. Down in the well. Very deep, going down, I was trying to catch some red thing, red dot, red circle. Some round thing was there, I was trying to catch it, went down, down. It was a black thing I could see from above and it was going down, down, down.

D: Describe this black thing.

C: [Using his hands to show a round motion with his hands] It's round and the red ball was going down and I was trying to catch it. It was like red ball with spots, spots, spots like this [pointing with the index finger and thumb], and it was going down like this. I could see it going down.

D: Describe that spot.

C: [Showing a round motion with his hands] It was round like this, was very bright red, it was going down . . . the black thing very fast.

D: What was the spot?

C: Some ring, round thing. [Showing a round shape with his hands] Red, it was red only. Red spots. Not spot. It was a red thing. I could see it going down in the black [making a downward motion of the hand]. I was trying to catch it; I could see it going down.

Here, we see that from multiple images, he keeps coming back to the red thing, and slipping down. He could not take this any further, so I asked him to do a few doodles.

Doodles

All of us have at some point in our lives got bored during a telephone conversation, and found ourselves scribbling in the corner of a sheet of paper, or even during a lecture, when we end up drawing some repetitive shape in a notebook. A doodle is a meaningless, rough design, drawing or abstract, which is produced aimlessly or absent-mindedly while preoccupied. It is highly improvised, irrational, illogical and unconnected to the external reality, and is generally done to pass time. The conscious attention is elsewhere, making the process of doodling only a partially conscious one. Hence, a doodle is clearly an expression of the subconscious state.

The interpretations of doodles are similar to dream interpretation. Interpretations of doodles not only take into consideration the drawing itself but also the line pressure in which they are drawn. There are two ways to understand a doodle. One is through the mind and one is through experience. A doodle is most significant when produced when the mind is turned off. It is precisely at the moment when the pen touches the paper that the sensations come to the surface.

After completing the doodle, the patient is asked to simply look at it, not to think, interpret or understand what is on the paper; in fact, he is asked not to use his mind at all. He is asked to observe what physical and mental experiences are triggered by just looking at the doodle. The doodle acts as a reflection of his inner pattern, and looking at it can bring the inner experience and sensation to the surface. Chetan was the only patient (of the three) whom I asked to draw doodles during the case taking.

CHETAN

The doodle helps us get to the core sensation of an individual. It is a very powerful tool in the homeopathic process, and allows the patient to be self-aware. Chetan made four doodles for me.

Doodle 1

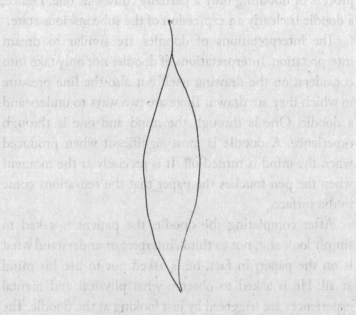

It is like a fish, half a body of a fish. I am trying to catch something—a light or something. It is going away. I have my hand outstretched towards it, I want this something. But it feels like I am in a cage or something. Bars are in front of me. It is a cage, which is keeping me from reaching something I want. I am trying to go against it. Something is stopping me. It's very near, but I am not getting it. Something is stopping me. Something black is there in front, it is not letting me get what I want.

Doodle 2

This is a square thing. It has many, many squares; square after square. There are squares after squares after each square. I am trying to go through it to get that thing. It is shining, but there is something black in front of me. It is like a tunnel of squares, and the thing there at the end is a bright thing, and I am not getting it. This bright thing is like a flame, an oval; it is a bright yellow, oval thing. I can see it but I cannot describe it properly. I try to go to it. It is a very thin kind of thing and tall. It is calling me towards it but I cannot get to it. There are a lot of birds there flying up and up, but that thing is going far away from me.

Doodle 3

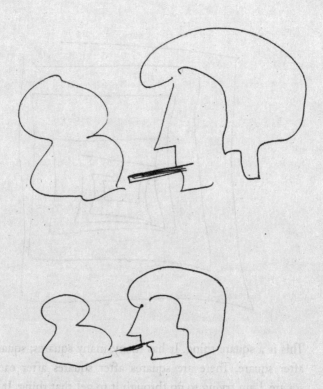

This is a face. It is a side face. I usually draw this image. It is all over my books. This is a boy who is enjoying. He is laughing and there is smoke all around. He is enjoying and sitting calmly with a cigarette in his hand. He is laughing, there is smoke all around. It is bad smelling. There is smoke everywhere. He has long black hair, smoking black. All this smoke is everywhere. He is very happy. He is very fat. Enjoying and sitting with his very fat stomach. He is hitting, hitting anyone who is coming near him. He is walking, he is very huge, and he is very fat. Everyone is afraid of him. He is walking on the road, wearing a jacket, with a bottle in his hand, and smoking. And anyone who comes in front of him, he kicks them. He has a big car. He is smoking. Fat. Very pot-bellied, everyone is looking at him. He is fetching into his jacket and pulling something out. He has a lot of money. He is pulling huge bags of money out. Everyone is walking with him, his friends. He is wearing nice clothes like a king.

He is now flying in an airplane; he is flying and flying, eating and smoking also. He is looking at everyone who is down there, and he is going up, up into the sky. He is doing various things in the sky, and comes down with a parachute to everyone congratulating him. He makes a round and round motion in the sky, it is like the figure 8 or something. He is going up and down, up and down, in this motion [here, Chetan was making a figure 8 design in the air with his hand]. It is like a sign of infinity, it is going up like this, like a roller coaster, and then down again. Everyone is looking up at him and he is making this figure 8. Everyone is looking at him, laughing and throwing things at him; he is enjoying. Everyone is congratulating him as he comes down, he is very famous and getting all the flowers and presents. Everyone is looking at him and he is getting the flowers, he is throwing the flowers to the crowd. He is feeling very happy and proud. Everyone is looking at him. He is feeling very good, above everyone, happy, on the top, no one can beat him. No one can do what he is doing. He is above everyone, on the top. He is happy and satisfied there, he is enjoying that moment and everyone is there with him. He is very fat, eating food and wearing good clothes.

He is wearing a jacket. It has stripes, red and white stripes. He has a cap with a red diamond on it. He is walking to his big red car, and there are girls all around him. They are everywhere. They are all tall, thin girls, with long golden hair. All are fair-looking, anaemic-looking. They are all thin, white-looking girls. Thin, long hair, and they are all around him. He is going in his red car, and everyone is running behind him. Everyone wants to get in the car. They all want to be with him, they are trying to get into the car. They want to laugh, enjoy, drink, and eat with him. They are running behind his car, the car is going up and down on the road. It is like a snake, going up and down, like a ribbon. It is again looking like a figure 8, going up and down, up and down. When it goes up you can see it, when it goes down, you cannot see it. And it repeats this over and over. This road is going on and on, and comes to a big cone-like thing.

Doodle 4

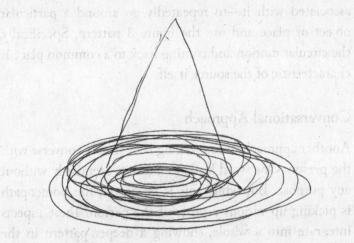

When he looked at this doodle, he said:

> They have reached the bright-red cone. It is bright and
> they are all moving around it. They are all happy because
> they have reached the cone. They are satisfied that they
> have gotten what they want. They are happy, laughing
> around the cone, going around the cone, and feeling peace.
> When they reach the cone, they feel calm and cool. They
> sit there forever, there is peace, they are happy and they
> are satisfied. They all sit around the cone, looking at the
> cone. Those who are sad—when they look at the cone,
> they become happy. They are walking around the cone, in
> circles. They are going around the cone, in circles [moving
> hands in circular motion].

Later on in our analysis, we will see that the remedy that Chetan needed has precisely this kind of movement associated with it—to repeatedly go around a particular object or place and use the figure 8 pattern. Specifically, the circular motion and coming back to a common place is characteristic of the source itself.

Conversational Approach

Another approach to case taking is to simply converse with the person. One word leads to another, seemingly without any purpose. But while this is going on, the homeopath is picking up various aspects of the person. These aspects integrate into a whole, showing a deeper pattern in the words that the person has been using.

I once looked over the case of a famous entertainment personality. He listed five of his complaints, and just said, 'Help me with these.' What he really meant was: 'That's it, I have nothing more to tell you.' When I asked him about his mood and state of mind, he said, 'It's perfect.' So I started to generally converse with him.

I tried to explain to him that it was important for him to know about himself, but he insisted that everything was okay for him, except these five listed problems. I realized that as long as he felt that I was probing, he was going to be reticent. So I took his list of complaints and placed it in my pocket and told him I would send him the medicine. Then I casually asked him, 'As a matter of curiosity, since you are involved in both television and the movies, is there a difference for an actor in these two mediums?' He said, 'Yes, of course. In television you are live and you have to be very alert. You cannot afford to make mistakes.'

Then he warmed up to this subject, because he felt that the medical case taking was over and this was just a casual conversation on a subject that was close to him. I took the clue and asked him what he meant by 'you could not make a mistake'. He said, 'Well, if you make a mistake, you risk losing your reputation that has been carefully built.' I asked him how that felt—to be in a situation with the risk of making a mistake and losing one's reputation—was it a stressful or an anxious situation? He said, 'I have gotten used to it, but initially I had a lot of anxiety in that situation because reputation is what an actor lives by. It is what makes him or breaks him.'

I further asked him why he felt that way, because was it really possible that a single mistake could damage a reputation? Then he started giving me examples from his life and from the lives of others, and slowly his perception of life and his sensitivity about his honour being wounded emerged. He told me about the various attempts by others to damage his reputation. The conversation ended up lasting well over two hours! From this I could gather how sensitive this man was, and I was able to identify his exact sensitivity and locate a remedy.

Another case which took shape just through conversation

was that of a lady with psoriasis. She talked about how she did not like the way her mother treated the servants. Then she said that her mother treated her as if she was insignificant. Later in the conversation she came to her fondness for pets, especially dogs. When I asked about her fondness for dogs, she said we should respect them. Then she compared dogs to cats and spoke for twenty-five minutes about cats—how graceful they were, and many other aspects. And so her life story went into a different space entirely!

Many times this conversation style helps the case to open up and the homeopath can get the whole story. Using this approach, the homeopath keeps touching upon different areas of the patient's life. From certain key words and the language the patient uses, the homeopath can then go to the next story and keep on connecting. The goal is to keep moving towards seeing the whole pattern at a deeper level.

Through these various techniques, a homeopath tries to get a glimpse into the experience or sensation of the patient beyond the barriers set up by the logical mind, which is full of theories and explanations. By looking at what comes spontaneously, without thinking, logic or reason, the homeopath is able to bypass the conscious mind of the patient and hear the language of the core inner experience.

15

ANALYSIS

The connecting thread of each individual through the various aspects of his life, as outlined above, is observed by the homeopath. This connecting thread is the innermost pattern or experience. This experience can be categorized as plant, mineral or animal experience. The pattern can be further differentiated into a specific plant family, mineral group or animal class.

Added to this, the symptoms of the patient, both mental and physical, are studied to find out which homeopathic remedy matches them. Often that remedy belongs to the exact kingdom the patient's pattern has otherwise indicated. It is as if each remedy reflects the song of the substance from which it is sourced, and as if the patient speaks the language of the source at the deepest level of his experience. This language, in terms of both the pattern and the symptoms, is taken into account to select the appropriate remedy for the patient.

That remedy is administered in an ultra-diluted form, which is termed potency (see chapter 1). It subconsciously produces an awareness of the situation and stimulates healing. Healing occurs in the person as a whole—physically, mentally and emotionally.

The process of analysis and remedy selection has been illustrated through the three case studies; one patient needs a plant remedy, the other a mineral remedy and the third an animal remedy.

BHARAT

The first step in the analysis for Bharat is trying to understand his basic experience that runs throughout each section of the case. What is the commonality that is illustrated?

When we try to understand his basic and core experience, what we see again and again is the presence of fear and terror, the need to escape or run away, with the reverse experience of numbness, violence, killing, death and rage. Right from his entry into the clinic we see his fearful nature (see chapter 5). Throughout the case-taking process and in all of the areas of Bharat's life, it was evident that there were elements of tremendous fear and panic, aggression, and a history of abuse from his father, all producing feelings of forsakenness, uselessness, sadness and vulnerability, resulting in an experience of becoming numb, frozen, and wanting to hide from everything and everyone.

Bharat is a very sensitive individual who is in a state of isolation, helplessness and deep despair. His dreams are frightful and scary, full of animals chasing him or of dead bodies, with the same feeling of being terrified. He cannot even watch television or movies because he is terrified of ghosts and skeletons, of the dark and especially being alone in the dark. He also has tremendous fear before interviews, exams or tests, and when people look at him.

As we have understood from the previous chapters, when a patient needs a remedy from the plant kingdom, they will have a universal experience of sensation and reaction or sensitivity and reactivity. This individual's nature and disposition tends to be soft, sensitive, emotional, sentimental, disorganized, adjusting, easily influenced, adaptable and irritable. The triggering factor of their problems is generally emotional or physical hurt and abuse, or some kind of shock.

This picture represents Bharat's case entirely. The whole issue of being terrified and frightened was a result of the violent, physical abuse he suffered from his father or others in childhood. This for him was a shock and his reaction was to become numb, frozen and terrified.

In summary, the main sensations in the case of Bharat include:
— Fear, fright, terror, panic
— Sudden violence
— Rage and aggressiveness
— Numbness, being stupefied, frozen, shocked

— Death, killing
— Being pursued, attacked
— Escape
— Desire to hide or run away

In the plant kingdom, there is one sub-family that shares these same experiences as Bharat. This is the *Solanaceae* family, which includes the potato, tomato and nightshade group.

Features of the *Solanaceae* Family

The *Solanaceae* family has a universal feeling that is common to all experiences. That is of being fearful, frightened and terrified.

The plants in this family have well-known sedative properties and have been used as anaesthetics and sedative drops. They produce extreme overstimulation of the sympathetic nervous system, which is known to cause all of the symptoms of fright—flight or fight—as listed below:

— Palpitations
— Trembling
— Dilatation of pupils
— Dryness of mouth
— Congestion (especially of head)
— Coldness in one body part with surges of heat in another

In Bharat's case, he used to experience palpitations, trembling, as well as coldness in one body part. In patients who need a remedy from the *Solanaceae* family, every mental stimulus is perceived to be frightening or threatening. The strategy is to suppress these instincts. The urges are strong but suppressed. As we have seen, Bharat is frightened and threatened by almost everything around him. This is his main experience.

Individuals who need remedies from this family experience life very intensely and vividly. This intensity is also seen on a physical level. For example, in all of the remedies of this family, there is violent rage, leading to destructiveness and a desire to kill. In Bharat's case record form, he had expressed an intense desire to kill, torture and beat his father. He wanted to break his father into tiny bits and pieces and kill him.

In summary, the main feeling of the *Solanaceae* family, and individuals needing medicine from this family, is of being abandoned in a dark, strange, dangerous place like a jungle where wild animals are ready to pounce upon them and eat them up. With pupils dilated and cold hands, they cling desperately to someone so that they are not left alone. They develop hypersensitivity and alertness to noise, in reaction to all the sensory changes around them, and as a protection against this fearful, dark world. Their fear of being abandoned makes them extremely sensitive to supposed insult or reprimand and they react with violence born out of terror and panic.

The following list is a summary of the *Solanaceae* sensations, active reactions and passive reactions. The sensation is what the person experiences. The passive reaction is how it affects the person and the active reaction is how he reacts to the situation. The ones that have been underlined are the main ones in Bharat's case:

Sensation

— <u>Violent</u>	— Shooting
— Splitting	— Sun strokes
— Bursting	— Apoplexy
— Explosive	— <u>Violent terror</u>
— Tearing	— <u>Pursued</u>
— Pulsating	— <u>Murder</u>
— Spasmodic	— <u>Killed</u>
— <u>Jerking</u>	— Themes of black and white
— <u>Constricting</u>	— <u>Light and dark</u>
— <u>Choking</u>	— <u>Life and death</u>

Passive Reaction

— <u>Anaesthetic</u>	— <u>Cowardice</u>
— <u>Stupefied</u>	— <u>Faintness</u>
— Lack of irritability	— <u>Stupor</u>
— <u>Sluggish</u>	— <u>Unconsciousness</u>

Active Reaction

— <u>Acute senses</u>   — <u>Striking</u>

— <u>Hurried</u>   — <u>Escape</u>

— <u>Shrieking</u>   — <u>Panic</u>

— <u>Startling in sleep</u> — Rage

— <u>Spasms</u>   — <u>Fright or flight reaction</u>

It is important to note that in both animal and mineral remedies, there are no active or passive reactions. In the case of minerals, they do not experience something happening to them: the issue is more of lacking or losing something. There is no direct action and reaction.

In animal remedies, the focus is on the survival mechanism, a whole intricate pattern of survival tactics. How the animal eats, walks, reproduces and defends is vital to understanding the complexity of the strategy for survival. Therefore, the question of reaction does not arise in animal remedies because something is not happening to them and they react to it, like in plant remedies.

Additional Words Used by Patients Who Need *Solanaceae* Remedies

— Violence   — Violent

— Killed, life and death   — Murder

- Pursued
- Horror
- Shock
- Terror
- Chase
- Fighting
- Attack
- Hit
- Beat
- Sluggish
- Analgesia
- Dead
- Stupefaction
- Flight
- Escaping
- Starting in sleep
- Screaming

- Sudden
- Fright
- Panic
- Terrify
- Aggression
- Brutality
- Show aggression
- Strike
- Stupefied
- Cowardice
- Numb
- Sedating
- Escape
- Run away
- Fight
- Spasms
- Rage

Along with this, we see a common theme in Bharat of isolation, seclusion and confinement. Also, he experiences an intense hopelessness about his situation, like oppression or deep despair. There is great contempt and disgust, aggressiveness and sadism, a loathing of life, and a general feeling that he is an outcast.

This type of personality usually feels that the situation is always very dangerous and hard to solve—it is hopeless.

Basically, the person would think of all the reasons why it is difficult or impossible. He feels like a total outcast: secluded, alone, isolated, stranded, and at the mercy of anything—robbers, strangers and even ghosts.

The remedy from the *Solanaceae* family that has this experience in addition to the main experiences of fear, fright and terror is called *Mandragora officinarum*. In this medicine, the main theme and sensation is of being 'disgusted by violence and rage'.

The name of the plant is mandrake, commonly known as Satan's Apple. The mandrake has a large brown root, which grows deep into the soil, about three to four feet.

The shape of the mandrake root, which often divides into two or more, gave rise to the belief that it resembled the human form. In olden times, it was thought that a powerful spirit inhabited the plant. The root contains hyoscine, a powerful alkaloid with the ability to cause hallucinations, delirium and, in larger doses, coma. It was the presence of this alkaloid, as well as the shape of the root, that led to the mandrake's association with magic, witchcraft and the supernatural.

Mandragora has traditionally been used as a sedative, painkiller or hypnotic in medicine at a time when there were no anaesthetics. It was used either as an infusion or something that could be smoked in order to lose consciousness or induce false death. However, if too much of it were to be ingested, the result would be fatal. Ingesting this plant causes a lot of numbness. It is believed

Natural Kingdoms

that a concoction of wine made from this root was given to Jesus at the cross.

Mandragora individuals are very passive and are very much in touch with their fears. They are unable to distinguish between one world and the other. They often have sleeplessness because they are afraid of their dreams. Usually, one of the main fears of *Mandragora* is confronting the living world rather than ghosts. They are much more scared of the material world. In Bharat's case, this was represented by his main complaint—of being unable to sleep (see chapter 7).

The idea of having control over their instinctual side is a huge issue in *Mandragora* individuals, represented by an alternation of symptoms, where they have to clench and restrain what might escape. There are many symptoms from the proving of *Mandragora* that resembled Bharat's state. There are delusions such as of being ignored, reproached unfairly by society, thought ugly, or is unloved or uncared for. There are dreams of deformity and disfigurement, of cruelty and mutilation. Mentally, there is an overwhelming sense of isolation, misanthropy and lack of sympathy.

Superficially, one might say that Bharat's situation is like that of a victim: his father was the aggressor, and he was the victim. Or, sometimes Bharat was the aggressor when he wanted to kill his father. It was a situation of Bharat versus his father, and so it could be a story of conflict and survival—thus needing an animal remedy.

Or we can see it as a relationship issue where Bharat was dependent on his father and his father let him down, and as a result, the issue was of a structure that had broken. However, in homeopathy, what is important is not what the situation actually was, but what it was perceived to be.

When Bharat was asked about his experience of the situation with his father, he did not say it was that of one versus another, or of dependence and the breaking down of his structure. He experienced terror, fear and panic as a sensitivity and reactivity to what his father was doing. It is this theme of fear and terror, and the sensitivity and reactivity, which are the connecting thread throughout this case.

All of us have these three qualities—sensitivity, issues of structure, and competitive or survival instincts. In fact, we should have all three! Each of these comes into play in certain situations.

The problem occurs when we are stuck in a specific pattern, which may be a pattern of sensitivity, structure or survival. Even though all of us have all three patterns, it is at the underlying level where we are stuck in one specific pattern. You can see in Bharat's case that he is stuck in a pattern where he reacts with fright and terror to every situation.

Take special note of the themes of the *Solanaceae* family that came up during the follow-ups. This confirmed the family and, ultimately, the remedy that was chosen.

DR ALI

Dr Ali came to see me for complete head-to-toe eczema, which he had had for forty years already.

Given his story and situation, or experiences in life, we need to understand what was behind all of this, what he experienced. How did he view life? When you come to the baseline, there were two things that were striking and vitally important for him.

The first was creativity. He had an incredible ability of playing with words, creating beautiful, romantic poetry. His creativity extended all the way to his theatrical voice, and in his reinterpreting religious texts and scriptures. As was clear from his case record form, the way he wrote in calligraphic handwriting, along with picturesque and complex poems, was also a part of his creativity.

Further, there was a certain dignity that he brought into his mannerisms and speech, as if he were on a pedestal. However, from his experience and expressions, one could fathom that he felt that he was unable to maintain that high position. At some point, he felt 'I am no longer needed, my creativity is not valued. I am an ex-professor. Now I get cheap and unimportant work, I am not even a shadow of what I should be or what my former self was.' This was the feeling he had of himself, which came across as a deep sense of inferiority, rejection or worthlessness. He often said, 'I don't get those assignments. I am a has-been.'

On the other side of this was a sense of absolute ego. It was like feeling 'I don't care, I know better. I don't care what anyone thinks of me. I will lead my own life.' There is an email in which he said, 'I wear rags. I buy my clothes at the street shops.' He was quite okay with this fact and appeared to be proud of it.

Dr Ali proclaimed that he was simple and spare. He had been wearing used clothes and did not care. He had lived life his way. He enjoyed being naked and free, but ensured that he drew the curtains for privacy. Moreover, the most striking thing about Dr Ali was his strong sense of criticism—right from the case record form, with the small corrections and additions, to the seeking out of misprints and errors. When I requested him to review a DVD lecture and also a book I had written, he reverted to me with a rather severe criticism of both. For Dr Ali, the pattern is of the mineral kingdom experience, where there is a lack, loss or fall of structure, position or performance.

Features of the Mineral Kingdom

Minerals have to do with structure. Structure can be understood in terms of existence, identity, position, relationships, security, performance and responsibility. We think of a mineral remedy in a case when the patient doesn't give a precise local sensation or gives many local sensations. These local sensations lead us to an issue of structure and organization; it is related to forming, maintaining or losing of this structure (be it relationships, performance, security, and so on). Every aspect of the patient's life can be narrowed down to such issues.

The issue is about 'completeness' or 'incompleteness' (expressed as something is missing or lacking) in the self or structure or a 'fear of losing that completeness'.

This is conveyed in patients as:

— Lack of identity   — Lack of stamina
— Lack of support   — Lack of confidence
— Lack of a relationship   — Lack of security
— Lack of position or power

Some Words Suggesting the Issue of Structure

— Affects functioning   — Fortify
— Bolstering   — Hampers working
— Breaking   — How far I can grow
— Build up   — Incapable to perform
— Cannot perform   — Lacking
— Collapsing   — Organized
— Crashing down   — Perfect
— Decaying   — Perfecting
— Deficiency   — Persevering
— Destroy   — Polished
— Disintegrating   — Polishing
— Endurance   — Precise
— Enhancing   — Pressurized
— Eroding   — Refining
— Fault within me   — Ruined

In mineral remedies, the problem is not with another person but always with oneself. For example, they would say, 'I have to bear with whatever he is doing to me only because I am not independent. If only I were complete, then there would be no problem. It is my insecurity that leads to problems.'

The mineral experience corresponds with the stages of human development that find their reflection in the seven rows[*] and eighteen columns of the Periodic Table of the Elements.

Group→ Period↓	1	2	3	4	5	6	7	8	9	10	11	12	13	14	15	16	17	18
1	1 H																	2 He
2	3 Li	4 Be											5 B	6 C	7 N	8 O	9 F	10 Ne
3	11 Na	12 Mg											13 Al	14 Si	15 P	16 S	17 Cl	18 Ar
4	19 K	20 Ca	21 Sc	22 Ti	23 V	24 Cr	25 Mn	26 Fe	27 Co	28 Ni	29 Cu	30 Zn	31 Ga	32 Ge	33 As	34 Se	35 Br	36 Kr
5	37 Rb	38 Sr	39 Y	40 Zr	41 Nb	42 Mo	43 Tc	44 Ru	45 Rh	46 Pd	47 Ag	48 Cd	49 In	50 Sn	51 Sb	52 Te	53 I	54 Xe
6	55 Cs	56 Ba	*	72 Hf	73 Ta	74 W	75 Re	76 Os	77 Ir	78 Pt	79 Au	80 Hg	81 Tl	82 Pb	83 Bi	84 Po	85 At	86 Rn
7	87 Fr	88 Ra	**	104 Rf	105 Db	106 Sg	107 Bh	108 Hs	109 Mt	110 Ds	111 Rg	112 Cn	113 Uut	114 Fl	115 Uup	116 Lv	117 Uus	118 Uuo

*	57 La	58 Ce	59 Pr	60 Nd	61 Pm	62 Sm	63 Eu	64 Gd	65 Tb	66 Dy	67 Ho	68 Er	69 Tm	70 Yb	71 Lu
**	89 Ac	90 Th	91 Pa	92 U	93 Np	94 Pu	95 Am	96 Cm	97 Bk	98 Cf	99 Es	100 Fm	101 Md	102 No	103 Lr

Source: Wikimedia Commons

---

[*] The sixth and seventh rows include a series of elements listed separately, namely, lanthanides and actinides.

Row	Issue
1	Existence, Birth
2	Separation
3	Identity, Care and Nourishment
4	Security and Task
5	Going into something new, Creativity and Performance
6	Responsibility
7	Disintegration

Once we see that a person's issues have to do with the mineral kingdom, that he feels a certain lack or loss within himself, then we can further classify what he feels he is lacking or losing.

People in the first row, which represents Hydrogen and Helium, feel that they lack their very existence. They describe their experience as 'I don't even know if I exist', 'Am I just a spirit, or am I a material body?' This is mentioned at the deepest level of the experience, not superficially. When you ask about their deepest experience of anxiety or grief, they will say, 'Do I really exist?'

Individuals needing medicines from the second row of the periodic table feel that they need to be protected by someone else. When you ask them what kind of protection they need, they may say, 'I need a cushion around me. I want to be enclosed inside a soft, protective covering, so I am not exposed to the outside world.' They often say, 'I want to be inside the womb.'

People who need the remedies from the third row of the periodic table, such as *Natrum* (Sodium) or Magnesium, feel that they lack, need, or are dependent on a very caring, nourishing relationship, such as the one given by an extremely close friend or parent. They also feel the need to develop their own identity, own choices and their own opinion, rather than just agreeing with what the other is saying.

Individuals who need remedies from the fourth row such as *Kali* (Potassium), Calcium or *Ferrum* (Iron) have a need for or are afraid of losing material security—money, physical protection, family, job, health, etc. They are highly concerned about their jobs and their bank balances.

People who need remedies from the fifth row seem to have gone one step further into creativity, performing, problem solving and innovating. These are scientists, musicians and artists. What they want to have is skill. What they are afraid to lose is their ability to perform, innovate or create.

In the sixth row of the periodic table, the issue seems to be the need to take on responsibility—firstly for themselves and then for those around them. They see their position as one of leadership, power and responsibility. They are afraid to lose this ability, position or power.

The seventh row represents the stage of disintegration and death. In the mineral kingdom, when the substances become too heavy to hold together, they start disintegrating and turn radioactive. For human beings, this symbolizes old age, where the body starts disintegrating and finally dies.

Thus, we can see the development of a human being reflected in the seven rows of the periodic table. The level at which a person seems to be stuck relates to the row that has his remedy.

Further, in the periodic table, remedies in the columns on the extreme left feel themselves capable of success. From the left to the middle, they are trying for success. In the middle, they are successful. On the right side, they are maintaining success. Towards the extreme right, they are failing and giving up success.

This information regarding the periodic table is only indicative and there is much more information and in-depth analysis that goes into the explanation of the periodic table and its application in homeopathy.

We have classified Dr Ali's experience into the mineral kingdom. The next step is deciding the row of the periodic table into which he fits. There are two polarities or dimensions of the case. One is of an esteemed professor with creativity, dignity and honour, and the other is of the person who wants to be who he is, wears rags and doesn't care what people think of him. The identity crisis within Dr Ali was very strong.

The main way we can understand this case is through his dream of a little girl watching him engage in sexual intercourse with his wife. The experience was that she was watching him with sinister eyes—he was afraid she would reveal his sexual act to the world. He felt people would then laugh at him, and he would lose his dignity and honour. As a result, he would be embarrassed and experience a sense of indignation. This was one side of the polarity.

The other side of this was that in the privacy of his own home he walked around naked. 'In my home, I want to be me; I don't want to wear clothes because society tells me to.'

Sometimes, a remedy from the periodic table is not a single element; if it is a salt, it can have two or more elements. For instance, common salt, sodium chloride, has both the elements from the third row. However, you can have a salt that has elements from two or more rows. In which case, you will see a unique interplay between the rows, as we see in the case of Dr Ali.

In Dr Ali, we are able to see that his ability to create, innovate, be an artist, performer and a distinguished professor reveals qualities of the fifth row. His need to assert his own choice and individuality shows us qualities of the third row. What can be understood from this is that he needs a medicine that is a salt, which has components from both the third and fifth rows.

In the fifth row, we see that Dr Ali perceives that he is

losing his position or ability. This puts him on the right side of the periodic table and in the fifth row, in the element of Antimony (fifteenth column). As we see from the above excerpt regarding Dr Ali's retirement and subsequent loss of capacity due to age, it is safe to say that he falls on the right side of the periodic table, where he is losing the structure that he had built.

We also see that he can be placed in the third row, where he wants to assert his own choices. Interestingly, Sulphur falls in the third row, which has the main themes of identity and ego. Clearly, Dr Ali has fully developed his identity, and which he has the fear of losing, and this again puts him on the right side of the table, leading us to Sulphur.

The sulphide of Antimony is called *Antimonium crudum*, a very common remedy in homeopathic practice. When we study this remedy in the homeopathic *Materia Medica*, it beautifully matches the picture Dr Ali presents. Incidentally, he also has many symptoms that appear like the remedy Sulphur.

The fifth row of the periodic table in homeopathic terms is known as the Silver Series. This row has to do with performance and creativity. The keywords representing this include: inventor, creation, inspiration, ideas, science, art, culture, unique, admiration, performance, aesthetics, beauty, show, ambition, queen and voice.

As seen from the numerous case examples above, these words are wholly representative of Dr Ali, the creative and gifted professor who loved to share his creations, ideas and culture, and desired admiration.

In the fifteenth column, the main themes are loss and going down. Here, the individual's structure is breaking, and he needs to be very careful, because the structure is being taken away. The structure is eroding and coming away in parts and its integrity cannot be preserved. This is the stage of loss where there is a disappearance of what has been achieved.

The keywords representing the fifteenth column include: lose, destroy, destruction, eject, loss, fall, defeat, going down, decay, surrender, abdicate, sacrifice, forgive, forget, poison, refusing, contrary, sudden, unforeseen, and over. As observed so far, Dr Ali feels he is in the evening of his life and is decaying.

In the remedy *Antimonium crudum*, the main feeling is of being let down and disappointed by others, therefore needing to narrow one's circle and isolate oneself. The *Antimonium crudum* patient finds the world around him so disappointing that he simply shuts it out and conjures up an illusionary, ideal world in which he starts living.

The main theme of this medicine is loss of fame, where the individual becomes silenced and a martyr. He longs for that which he misses or has been disappointed by: he becomes nostalgic and longs for his native land, for the ideal woman—the woman of his dreams. He becomes poetic and sentimental. Poetry often expresses his inner wishes. He is lost in this idealization.

Individuals who need this remedy are prone to writing 'verses'; they make rhymes and write poetry. They are known to be sentimental individuals, who desire the idealistic realities, and they are nostalgic and long for the past. They theorize and fantasize. All of these symptoms of *Antimonium crudum* matched Dr Ali's total mental picture.

The individuals who need *Antimonium crudum* feel they are going to lose their creativity and, along with it, also lose the love and respect of their friends and family. So they always have to be different, to produce something that goes against all common expectations, if only to catch attention and make sure people still notice them.

They may start to look for compensation for their loss of fame, by building a romantic picture of love. They may experience a poisoned relationship if they start to think that their partner is trying to silence them and stop them from doing what they want. They have a tendency to wear attractive clothing, but when they feel unloved they develop a preference for wearing shocking clothes. When they think their talents are not appreciated any more, they go against the grain.

Sulphur is a mineral remedy whose main symptoms include theorizing and fantasizing. Sulphur is an egotist and this ego is manifested as foolish happiness and pride. He thinks of himself as a great person and everything that he possesses appears to be beautiful.

Sulphur is indifferent to his own personal appearance

and also to the opinion of others. He is not disturbed by uncleanliness. Sulphur patients are known as 'ragged philosophers', who speculate and theorize on religious or philosophical subjects. Often, philosophers, scientists, religious magnates, great writers, poets and artists are akin to this remedy.

In Sulphur the main feeling is that of being scorned, suppressed, put down and criticized; where the person is made to feel humiliated and his pride is hurt, and he will do anything to avoid embarrassment. There is a tendency to boast and exaggerate, which boosts his ego. Being 'egotistical', 'overcritical' and 'censorious' does not earn him many friends. Having a background of knowledge with intensity and vastness, it is natural for him to develop a sort of 'pride' or superiority complex.

The symptoms of Sulphur that matched Dr Ali's include a history of skin eruptions, foolish, happy and proud behaviour, indifference to personal appearance, desires appreciation, and a critical, censorious nature.

CHETAN

This was the case of twenty-one-year-old Chetan. His main problem was Behçet's syndrome, causing ulcers in the mouth and on the scrotum. On observation, the most interesting thing was his amazing amount of energy. Everything he seemed to do was so fast in speed and pace, and constantly changing.

His manner of speaking was impulsive, hasty and hurried—almost hyperactive—and he would rapidly move his hands about at all times (see chapter 5). He used many emphatic hand gestures during the case taking as well, including rolling his hands over one another. Most frequently seen was his aggressive poking of his index finger into his palm of the opposite hand.

In Chetan's case, I found the deepest experience to be that of competition, one-upmanship, heightened sexuality, and animated, alluring and attention-seeking behaviour. These features closely resemble the animal kingdom experience.

Features of the Animal Kingdom

— Competitiveness
— To be ahead of others
— Superior vs Inferior
— No one else can be with me
— Someone I know tries to win, competing with me

— Need to attract
— Peak of the mountain
— At the top
— Deceit, malice, jealousy
— Sexuality

The following examples from Chetan's case that matched the animal kingdom themes include his feelings of inferiority, as if he knew nothing, was a zero, and the opposite feeling of being superior and number one—the boss. Jealousy was also present in his case, where he would become jealous if he lost to his friends, or if they were healthier or financially better off. He wanted to hit them but could not.

Chetan often hit and bit himself. He felt betrayed by his friends, which to him was like being stabbed in the back. He felt his friends had cheated him, and made a fool of him. He also liked to do things very fast, and to be quick and witty in order to be on top. Chetan had a big desire to win, to be the best and better than others, else he would feel inferior to them.

He also had heightened sexuality and thought about girls quite often—we see this not only in his everyday conscious experiences, but also in his unconscious experiences (dreams, doodles and meditation). He had uncontrollable feelings for one girl in particular, and had dreams where she had become pregnant by another. Chetan also lied a lot and could not control it.

Everything that Chetan said during the case taking pointed to the animal kingdom. The next step was to establish the kind of animal or class of animal to select his remedy from. The question was whether Chetan needed a medicine from the mammal group, reptiles, birds, molluscs or fish, or spiders or insects. This could be ascertained through his energy as well as his meditative journey.

During his meditation, he gave various images and phrases to represent his gesture of forcefully poking an index finger into the palm of the other hand. He gave descriptions of birds, mountains, flowers, a shell, a diamond, a snake, something red slipping down and down, but finally he settled on an insect, like a scorpion or a spider.

This led me to investigate the insect group.

Characteristics and Themes of Insect Individuals

- Impulsive, hurried
- Restless, hyperactive
- Busy/Industrious
- Quick
- Suddenness
- Moving, wandering talk
- Talks fast
- Too many wandering and rapid thoughts
- Feeling belittled, insulted, humiliated, disgusting, low and looked down upon
- Greedy, selfish and materialistic
- Irritable, annoyed, impatient

- Violence, knife, kill
- Cruel, destructive
- Shoot
- Burning like fire
- Breaking, hitting
- Shameless

- Increased sexuality
- Feeling of being small

- Feeling powerless, helpless

- Rude, sarcastic, vindictive, revengeful

196

The qualities of the insect sub-kingdom very clearly matched Chetan's.

We noted his impulsive, hurried, restless and quick nature. We also recognized his wandering speech and his fast pace of talking. We saw examples of his increased sexuality and acting unabashedly in the understanding of the kingdom.

The following examples from his case complete the insect characteristics of violence, cruelty, destructiveness, breaking, burning and hitting. When he was studying for his exams, he kept thinking his mother would get breast cancer. His own condition, too, made him fear he would get cancer or the parts would become gangrenous.

Chetan would get irritated and angry very quickly at those who he thought were trying to outsmart him, win over him and beat him. He felt like breaking things, hitting things, hitting his head on things, or even biting himself. He had broken pencils, he had hit the wall and the bed, and even himself.

Interestingly, he hated movies with fighting or killing in them. He did not like the idea of killing or being stabbed in the back. He felt it was very cruel, destructive and violent. He gave an example of people being killed very cruelly, like in a gas chamber. They would be burning and be on fire, and then someone would come to shoot them with guns.

Sensations of the Insect

— Pricking	— Striking
— Poking	— Poking with a sharp needle
— Stinging	— Sharp
— Hand gesture showing pointed finger	— Stitching

In Chetan's case, the sensations of the insect group matched perfectly. The poking and stitching sensations, along with his characteristic hand gesture of using his index finger to poke his palm, all indicated an insect remedy. The insect sub-kingdom was now confirmed. The next and final step was to find the insect source that Chetan needed.

The source of the medicine was found in the experiences of the series of doodles that he made. Through these doodles, the animal kingdom and the insect sub-kingdom characteristics were reconfirmed. For example, we saw issues of competitiveness, attractiveness, sexuality, being superior and not inferior, being the best and on top, and jealousy.

On closely investigating his doodles, his focus came to the figure-8 movement and a red cone. He described these figure-8 movements beautifully and traced them in the air with his hand as he explained the doodles.

This overall picture led me to understand that Chetan needed a medicine from the insect sub-kingdom which had this figure-8 movement and circular, rapid motion as a survival technique, and this is what I found:

> When a bee returns from a rich, new food source, it will communicate this information to other bees by a waggle dance. A waggle dance consists of one to 100 or more circuits, each of which consists of two phases: the waggle phase and the return phase. Excited by her discovery, she scrambles into her hive's entrance and immediately crawls on to one of the vertical combs. Here, amidst a massed throng of her sisters, she performs her dance.
>
> *This involves running through a small figure-8 pattern* [emphasis mine]: a waggle run (or waggle phase) followed by a turn to the right to circle back to the starting point (or return phase), another waggle run, followed by a turn and circle to the left, and so on in a regular alternation between right and left turns after waggle runs.[1]

The waggle phase of the dance is the most striking and informative part of the signalling honeybee's performance. This resembles the figure-8 pattern and circular movements that were present in Chetan's case.

Apis mellifica (prepared from the honeybee) is a homeopathic medicine given to individuals who are childish, foolish and immature; who have a feeling that others are laughing at and criticizing them, resulting in feeling left out. The individual who needs this medicine is trying to find individuality within the group. There is a desire to be mature and to be a great person. These individuals are jealous and competitive in a childish way. They behave in a way that attracts attention; they are extremely excitable, very hyperactive and cheerful.

Apis mellifica being the queen bee can be the most animated talker and have a vivacious but dominating personality. These patients talk in a hurried, busy, restless and uninhibited or shameless manner. They have wandering and a rush of thoughts and enjoy constant, intense activity.

Symptoms of the honeybee that match Chetan's characteristics include:

— Ailments from jealousy	— Burning heat
— Desire to break things	— Stinging
— Busy	— Biting
— Censorious and critical	— Stitching
— Cheerfulness, gaiety, happiness	— Stinging
— Childish behaviour	— Shifting
— Desire for company	— Excitement and excitability
— Disposition to contradict	— Lasciviousness, lustfulness
— Delusion that he is falling	— Nymphomania
— Delusion that he is enlarged	— Restlessness, nervousness

— Destructiveness   — Constant motion

— Dictatorial, domineering,   — Poking pain
dogmatic, despotic

After coming to the conclusion that Chetan could indeed need a remedy prepared from the honeybee, I went over his doodles once more, amused at how at a certain angle the doodle of the squares within the squares resembled the pattern of a honeycomb; the doodle of the cone looked almost like an inverted beehive with something circling very rapidly around it; and, lastly, there was a clear figure-8 pattern within the doodle of the smoking boy who was wearing a striped jacket. He had also written a very coincidental thing in the chief complaint section of his case record form: 'Discharge from ulcers is sticky, transparent, odour is sweet like honey.'

16

WHAT HAPPENED
AFTER THE REMEDY

The process of healing through homeopathy is a unique one. A remedy doesn't act locally but on the vitality of the patient, stimulating healing. There are changes not only in the patient's pathology and physical symptoms, but also a dilution of the embedded pattern that has ruled the patient's entire life. The patient experiences healing as freedom from a predetermined way of perceiving and reacting to situations, being more in the present moment. There is a change in his entire way of living and relating to the world. The process is gradual but long-term.

Each time the homeopath sees the patient, he has to assess and carefully evaluate what has happened with the given dose. He needs to consider a number of questions—does the person need the same or a different remedy; does he need a repetition of the medicine, or an increase in potency, and so on? Simply going to the pharmacy and taking a dose does not help.

This is illustrated through the follows-ups with the patients reproduced here.

BHARAT

The first follow-up I had with Bharat was through email, two months following his case taking:

Dear Doctor,

I had come for my case taking in February and it is now March. I was told to write you. There has been fractional and gradual improvement in sleep. A very old original symptom of sweating in the palms had come back in a small way, but now it has disappeared and they are back to being freezing cold as earlier. There is a small, but not significant change in my dreams; I still see snakes, dogs, threats, sex, disappointments and bad/sad dreams.

I used to have great difficulty to cry (it was actually impossible), but now I am able to do so without much difficulty. I had an incident at the office two weeks ago where I cried quite easily after a supervisor had been disrespectful.

I still feel an intolerable amount of frustration and anger. I have an extremely strong sensation to break and smash everything around me. I simply don't want to leave anything unbroken anywhere. I want to hurt/kill, cause huge amounts of pain and suffering to anyone and everyone who is not good to me.

These are my deepest sensations and I have had them for over two decades. I have never actually shown real violence and am actually considered to be mild. But deep within me lies a raging tornado that I have kept suppressed and hidden for so many years and even forgotten. When I came home from the case taking in February, I realized you were looking for something specific—which is my sensation.

In general, I am not as bad as I was before February.

I received the following email from Bharat four months into his treatment.

Dear Doctor,

My complaints I came with are slightly but surely better. People who have known me since long tell me that they see a small change and improvement. I also feel this.

My concentration is better, but still not good. My feelings of irritability, anger, frustration and the very deep sensations to break everything and hurt/abuse/kill everyone around are still largely present.

The place where there is most improvement is my mood and state of mind. My horribly low mood is now slightly better and for the very first time in life I am beginning to feel some peace within. I seem to be a little better in dealing with stressful situations than earlier.

I am slightly better since the last follow-up.

After five months of treatment, Bharat sent me another email.

Hello Doctor,

Life continues to be a struggle. It is just a challenge to be alive as I remain in a deeply disturbed state of mind. A good part is that I am better by a good 10 per cent since I started in February.

Also, there is an improvement in the throat. Before I could not consume any chilled/cold food and had to keep off of oily foods (ice cream was an absolute no), as they would drastically affect my throat. Now, I can use a little more oil in food and have slightly cold/chilled food without badly affecting my throat.

My mood is not as horribly bad as before and better by 10 per cent. I continue to live on the edge at all times and I am always ready to break down and cry. A plus or improvement here is that the crying now comes more easily.

As always I simply cannot handle stressful situations, but it is certainly not as bad as before coming to you. Just a few days back I had suddenly started to sleep better, which had resulted in a general better feeling. This is also better by 10 per cent.

A letter I received from Bharat six months into the treatment:

Dear Doctor,

All of my decades-old complaints/problems I have been suffering from are all better now. Last time I had reported a 10 per cent change since the beginning. Now, I can say it is between 15–20 per cent. My sleep, which had earlier shown no progress at all, is better by 15–20 per cent. I am not as terribly serious-looking and my facial appearance is less tense.

There are no new complaints. My terrible and unacceptable bad/poor mood is now not so bad and I have gained a bit of confidence. The way I deal with stress is much better than before.

I had a dream that my dreadful dad was alive; he came back. I was terrified and scared to have him around again. However, for the first time in my life, I am starting to feel some peace deep inside. . . .

Many, many thanks for bringing about improvement in my life.

After eight months of treatment, Bharat wrote me an email.

Dear Sir,

Most of my symptoms appear to be better than the previous time. During the case taking I had reported feeling massive headaches and heaviness, and undesirable deep disturbances in the mind. Now all of it is so much better and bearable in comparison.

My feelings of hopelessness, worthlessness, sadness and dullness are all better. My concentration is better, although I still cannot watch TV and read. I still do not go out, except to the office.

When I compare my moods and mind state with before, it is so much better. Difficult and tough situations have always taken a huge toll, especially on my emotional/mental health. Although it is still difficult, I am able to handle them better than before.

Previously I had reported starting to feel some peace deep within me and I still continue to feel this peace. In addition, I find some clarity in my thinking.

The medicines are working slowly but surely. I guess that decades-old chronic complaints cannot be expected to disappear in just a few months and I am grateful and thankful for the changes which have come so far.

After nine months, he wrote to me again.

Dear Sir,

I feel a shade better in comparison. Getting myself to do the simplest of tasks is a huge challenge, but it is not as tortuously difficult as it used to be.

I am still very scared to look at myself in the mirror—hugely thin, bony, shockingly dull, serious-looking and sad at times, even a bit scary. On my brighter side, I am at least over 20 per cent better than I have ever been—especially my feelings, and calmness within. I feel an overall 20 per cent + better since the beginning. This is higher than the 15–20 per cent reported [three] months back.

On the way home from my last night at the office after six years, I found myself crying endlessly the entire day and following night. The last time I had been able to cry like this was eighteen years ago after the incident with my father—which I described to you in the original case taking—when he thrashed me around like a dog.

The way I deal with stressful situations now is also a shade better. All of my life I have never been able to look up at a girl, but I can now sometimes manage to look at a girl (although rarely but surely). I find it impossible to smile back.

I am so very thankful for the sharing and endlessly grateful to be receiving medicines from your clinic.

After ten months of treatment, Bharat sent me another email.

I see a lot of improvement in most of the things. My headaches are so much better. The pain in my limbs is 50 per cent better. . . .

Overall, compared to many months back, I am 30 per cent better since treatment.

Now, I get sleep. I had no sleep for the past twenty years. I recently had a dream of my father, and he was actually good to me in the dream. I couldn't believe it. Now I want to meet his relatives and want to understand him. I want to understand about him and his childhood, and make the effort to do this.

After a year and two months, Bharat emailed me his follow-up.

Dear Sir,

All of my symptoms are hugely better. The most important symptom of sleeplessness is massively improved. I am now able to watch TV channels and have a better concentration span.

I have a better appetite and my long-standing problem of lack of thirst has gone. I freely drink lots of water and it feels very satisfying. I used to be very scared and terrified to look at myself in the mirror, but now I don't have much of a problem. My face appears to be much more relaxed in comparison.

I have started to look at girls a bit too much. In fact, I cannot take my eyes off of them even while riding in traffic. I tend to stare at them like there is nothing else more interesting and like they have never been around for me to look at anytime before in my life. Perhaps I will get over this fantasy once I start mingling/talking to them and make some friends.

My mood and state of mind are getting better by the week. My dullness and sad feelings are nowhere as severe and extreme as when I had started. My concentration, although still difficult and poor, is several times better, and now it is a bit safer when I ride on busy roads. I am still very scared, frightened and fearful, but only about half as much as earlier. Now I am seeing difficulties as opportunities to become stronger. I am even dealing with stress better than last time. I even had a dream I was with a girl and we had an intimate experience together.

I feel better than anytime before. I was able to watch a full movie in the theatre. Before, my concentration would drift away often. I managed to follow most of the movie, it felt so good. I hadn't been to a theatre in a very long time.

Continuous repetition of my medicine has been bringing great relief. I am glad to report that I am overall better by about 45 per cent. I am extremely satisfied with my progress and feel confident that with time I will eventually get close to being fully well. Please feel free to use my videos and emails in any of your seminars and training sessions. I do not have issues with people knowing me.

After two years, Bharat came to the clinic to see me to tell me about his current state of health.

Talking about my current state: after a horror-filled life right from childhood through to adulthood, after taking *Mandragora*, I have experienced a transformation. I feel pretty safe and sound, enjoy a good degree of mental peace, and I am quite good at my new job where I help colleagues every day.

People who had known me from my past express disbelief and surprise when they meet me! My very own brother, who wasn't speaking to me earlier, and his wife were a bit stunned when we ran into each other at a gathering recently. Then I visited their home and now I keep getting calls from them asking me to revisit!

It is as though the medicine literally changed my chemistry for good. I feel like growing it in my back yard, so I can see, touch and admire it every day.

It is so amazing that the little white sugar pills, which seemingly contain nothing at all, can give someone a new life!

With my deepest and ever-lasting gratitude.

From a terrorized, nervous, isolated being, Bharat literally flowered into a happy, smiling and socially confident young man.

DR ALI

Dr Ali hardly came to the office for follow-ups. He would telephone the clinic for his follow-up appointment and then pick up his medicine. For the first three months, there was slight improvement in his skin and we kept repeating the medicine. However, we finally saw him in the clinic four months after administering the remedy. He reported the good news.

I am improving—unless it is a very protracted phase of remission which is unlikely in the sense that if it were remission I would not feel different subjectively. I have started feeling different subjectively.

You know, in the lowest part of the mind the disease

211

has taken a turn and all sorts of symptoms are undergoing alleviation, including ones which probably I had not even shared with you. The typical sneeze is there once in a while. It is a very pleasant kind of sneeze and one feels as if it is catarrh. It has nothing to do with the seasonal cold kind of sneeze.

The tone of my skin has also changed and this is something which others have been sort of pointing out; those who have known me over a period of a quarter of a century. And those who have been witness to this torture, which was quite visible in the sense that I used to have scales on my face, fingers and toes. And I have been taking only your medicine—nothing else.

I have not been taking anything for the peripheral neuritis either. That persists, the neuritis, but then without medication I think that too is even behaving in a small measure.

And I have been eating virtually everything, which I was prohibited from earlier. It doesn't affect me in any way, whereas earlier on if I consumed an egg at breakfast, for four days in succession I would feel that somehow my skin would start reacting and now I must avoid it for a fortnight or so. I think I have been taking eggs every day for virtually three months at breakfast, and now I have nothing at all.

I feel as if the therapy is taking me along to the mysterious recesses of childhood and probably reminding me of some landmark, some fossil, somewhere like that. It is a kind of slow journey back; like I feel I got a slight patch for eight days on a part of my foot. This is something I used to have when I was a resident student, in the same location. And the aggravation, which you hinted at, is nothing in comparison with what I suffered from earlier with aggravation under half a dozen homeopaths. You feel a little uneasiness for a couple of days and then it sort of fades out, that kind thing. So the patches are there, the roughness is on the parts of the body, but quite manageable. I have not experienced the fit with which you know I used to wake up in the morning, go to the dining table and just go on rubbing my fingers for twenty minutes until they became moist. Like that kind of spasm and itching, and then it would subside and I would go back to sleep. Then when I got up in the morning, I would feel drained because of the itching—this has gone completely.

I have been walking about seven to eight kilometres a day at a slow pace, but I am walking. Once in a while when this is hurting, I slow down. But that incapacitating neuritis is very infrequent now.

Dryness has decreased remarkably. The feeling of dryness in the mouth and the dryness everywhere on the periphery has decreased. Before, it was as if I had been exposed to the sun all the time. Similarly, I have by way of an experiment, exposed myself to the sun. But the exposure to the sun did not in any way precipitate a bout of itching or anything at all. I have deliberately been in situations where there was a lot of dust and smoke. I inhaled it deliberately to see whether it triggered an attack. It didn't.

So, it is a very slow and steady kind of withdrawal of the symptoms. So I wouldn't use the word alleviation because that sounds rather temporary and that it may relapse. The cracks on my lips have diminished; perceptibly I can see in the mirror. My wife can feel it by running her finger on it. Otherwise it would be flaky and if you did not take precaution there would be scaling on the lips also.

I think I am easy with myself. I can work more. I can read more without my eyes feeling dry. I can write more. I can withstand the stress of say commuting to the centre of the city in the morning, coming home, taking my lunch, and going back to the city. This used to give me spells of itching and not feeling at ease. I would also get restless in the evening after a normal bath. Now it is not like this.

I am about 30 per cent better with the medicine. I feel that this treatment has restored my faith in homeopathy because I used to be very, very indignant at homeopathy. In fact, I used to tell ten people that this is the disease which homeopathy gifted to me, so beware of this therapy. Otherwise, I used to suffer from dermatitis seasonally, a patch here, a patch there. Homeopathy made my disease systemic. I was oozing all over. My trousers were wet, my shirts were wet, my sleeves were dripping, and when I showed the doctor, he would say, that means it is working! When he couldn't control this he put me on steroids. I thought: What kind of therapy is this? With your spoonful of water, this is the effect, which means a miracle!

I spoke with Dr Ali on the telephone after eight months of treatment.

> I am having a mid-day aggravation. I also had a mild rhinitis attack. There was dryness. The progress has been steady, and I have been otherwise fine. Mentally, I am okay and my energy levels are good. I had a dream of participants in a seminar appreciating me. Nothing weird is happening as such. I have never felt so buoyant!

After nine months of treatment, I spoke to him on the telephone for his follow-up.

> My skin has again gotten worse. For the first 8 months, it was improving. However, even though it is worse, the duration of the attacks is much less than past attacks.

I spoke with Dr Ali on the telephone for his follow-up after ten months of treatment.

> My skin is definitely better than last time. But the visitors did not notice. Generally, I am okay. I am 90 per cent better in appearance, but I am feeling the same distress. My face is okay now. So are my hands. There are scales, but it is better. My neuritis is also better. I have only had three attacks in the past four months. There is dryness in the folds of my skin and I have developed swelling in my fingers.

After a year, he came to the clinic to update me on his condition.

> Overall, my skin is much improved over the last year. The peripheral neuritis too is better and the swelling in my fingers is also much better.

Dr Ali called me on the telephone to follow-up after a year and two months.

> I went to Rajasthan and there was a good thing. I did not have any flare-ups. Usually when I go there, I get aggravated, but this time I did not. My peripheral neuritis is continuously getting better and I am able to walk faster! There is no itching or oozing of my skin, and generally I am feeling very good. I am gradually improving. I had a milder cycle for about ten days. This has been the mildest cycle so far. I did not stress at all about it. The dryness is so smooth now. This has happened for the first time in two years. I am now okay, and there are no skin troubles.

After a year and six months, I did a telephone follow-up with Dr Ali.

> Gradually, I am improving. It is like I am seen and I am going to be coming out of the shadows. My neuritis is better, and I can do my work faster. I can walk faster and there are no flashes of pain. My fingers are very soft now.

I again spoke with Dr Ali on the telephone after a year and nine months.

This is only the second flare-up I have had in the past four months. There is a yellowish coating on my tongue too. I am sensitive to taste. I have started to get an eruption on my upper lip and chin. The neuritis is better and I am not stressed. There is much less itching too.

On my fingers and neck there was a slight rash. It lasted ten to eleven days. It was like a beehive, so rough! The face had so much roughness. I am having dryness of the mouth, and my tongue is oversensitive. The anterior portion of the tongue is red and has cracks.

After two years, he came into the clinic for his follow-up.

I have eruptions at the nape of my neck, and they are filled with pus. I have cracks on my fingers—this hasn't happened since the last eight months. My face is burning and it feels raw. Also, there is a rash around my navel. My appetite is good. There is a sensation of pins and needles on my feet, but they are not painful. There is a painless ulcer on my tongue as well. The colouring has improved since last time. My mood is okay.

Two years and three months later, he reported his condition on the telephone.

The rash around my neck is persisting. There is also dryness around the neck. This is since the last one and a half months. The flaking is not as much, but my skin is looking like that of an elephant. It is not itching, but it gets worse with perspiration, dust and sun exposure. I have no stress and my cough has decreased.

From the last few follow-ups, we see that Dr Ali's improvement had plateaued. So we increased the potency of the medicine. After two years and six months, we followed up with him over the telephone.

My skin is better again. There is less scaling of the skin. However, I am getting involuntary twitching in my fingers sometimes. I am getting dryness and itching in the neck, face and palms, and vesicles are developing but it is not as bad as it was before. My legs are paining and get stiff. I need to walk with a support. I have developed an itching around my anus. But I have had no rashes or inflammations. The dryness around my neck and face has improved. And the fingers also; now it is only dryness and two or three cuts. The skin on my face is also better; it does not have any itching. Overall, I am better than last time by 30 per cent. My sleep is also very good.

We followed up with Dr Ali by telephone after three years.

My face is clear for the first time. I occasionally have the itching in the anus, but it has improved. The dryness around my neck and navel are both better. My sleep has become just okay, and my toes again are getting numb when I walk, but not as bad.

After three years and six months, I spoke with Dr Ali over the phone.

I am itching much less. My rash has quite improved. Everything seems better—my peripheral neuritis, my sleep and skin are all better. Overall, I say I am 50 per cent better. I have started cycling, about fifteen to twenty kilometres. There is no stress or tension! On the positive side, there has been no serious, full-blown attack for the past four years. The intensity is not there. Sometimes, I do suffer from restlessness or itching, but the skin is so much improved.

After five years, Dr Ali came to the clinic and reported a large difference from the first day we had met.

I am better than last time. The itching is almost gone. My energy levels are also very good. My complaints have improved considerably. The only rash persisting is around my navel and even that is better. I have a painful cyst in my right eye as well that has been troubling me for years. I have itching in both my ears.

My mood has been very good. There is no stress. I went to Goa, and with the rain, my itching increased. However, when I returned back to Bombay, I got better.

I am now working with utmost involvement and enjoying the work very much.

Eight years on, Dr Ali dropped by the clinic to inform me that he had been perfectly well for the past several months. His skin problems had completely disappeared. I saw that his face, which earlier had a whole flare-up of eczema, was completely clear, as was the rest of his body. His other complaints, such as his peripheral neuritis, were also gone. He was in the best of health, both mentally and physically, and looked several years younger. He and I both felt he did not need medication any longer.

When I requested permission in writing from Dr Ali to allow me to use his case in this book, he wrote:

I deem it as a modest contribution to the mission of reinstating homeopathy centrestage in the pantheon of Lord Dhanvantari [Hindu god of health] from where it was wrongfully exiled.

CHETAN

I met Chetan after a month for his first follow-up appointment. He told me that the pain in the testicular region was gone. There was slight itching and the ulcers were there but very few. Most of them had healed nicely.

On the right side of his testicles, the ulcers had gone. But ulcers were still there on his tongue. They were the same, but now he didn't think about them. Earlier, he used to think about them a lot, and worry about what might happen to him and his health. They were not painful.

He also reported that now he had much fewer dreams and his sleep was less disturbed. He had begun to get sound sleep, and in all, it was a very good month. He also explained that there was this tension when he had originally come, and even that had reduced a lot. He was enjoying much more with his friends, and had become very busy working. He said that his complaints had overall reduced as well as the palpitations.

He further explained:

In all ways things are good. My relationship with my parents has also improved and with friends, things have improved a lot. I have stopped eating non-vegetarian food. The tension about my health problems, like will I be better or not, will they go or not . . . this has all reduced, so I am feeling good! The pain has reduced. There was insecurity, like what will happen next. Even that has reduced now. Now I feel I will get cured!

The dreams I am getting are pleasant. Before they used to disturb me a lot. I feel refreshed in the morning when I wake up. I don't feel tired at all.

My energy level is good. Compared to before, I feel like working a lot. Study-wise too I have improved. Now I remember things in a much better way than I used to do earlier. I now can explain things in a better way. Like subjects which were difficult for me earlier, now they have become simple, because now I concentrate on them properly. At first, there were always persistent thoughts about my disease, which used to not help me. I wasn't conscious in what I was doing, and it used to not allow me to concentrate. Therefore, these thoughts of my disease and complaints used to continuously hamper me.

Here, Chetan showed the same gesture with his hand, poking his index finger aggressively into his palm. I asked him to repeat this gesture over and over, and explain what it was. He said,

It is like this is a disturbance. It used to come again and again. I used to think about it again and again. But now, that has gone. The disturbance has reduced by 70 per cent. I can put things in a better way. I am happy and I can explain to people what is going on. There also used to be a lot of restlessness. I used to keep thinking constantly what would happen next? How will I be in the future? What will I be? This thing has gone now. I am very happy with the treatment.

After four months of treatment, Chetan sent us an email.

I am feeling generally better. My USG is normal and the ulcers on the tongue are slowly going. The acne on my back and legs is getting better. My confidence has also increased more. There are no new scrotal ulcers to report.

I spoke on the phone with Chetan to follow-up after seven months of treatment.

> I currently have a bout of tonsillitis. The pain is pricking and is worse when I swallow. I had one dream of going to the hospital. I was being pricked by a needle. There is one ulcer that has come on my scrotum, but it is much better than before. It is not itching like before.

After twelve months of treatment, we received an email from Chetan.

> My eruptions are better. I am still having knee pain and head pain only sometimes. I am dreaming that I am in a relationship and have developed my confidence. My anxiety about the future is still there and I keep getting many thoughts about my future. I have a fear of failure. Overall, I see a great improvement in both my scrotal ulcers and mouth ulcers.

I last spoke with Chetan for a follow-up after he had undergone five years of treatment.

> I do not get disturbing dreams any more like before. My sleep has improved and the palpitations have gone. I am working very hard and my productivity has increased a lot. I have a wife now. I am married and settled in New York. I am confident and I can convince anyone. No one rejects me now. Everyone wants to work with me. I feel very good after the treatment.

My appetite is good and I have put on some weight. My sleep is one thing that has been very good. I do get dreams, active ones, but not disturbing ones. Generally, I am so much better. I feel refreshed for the first time in years.

My impression of too much hard work and busy-ness have decreased. I have been able to give more time to my family.

I feel I am excelling in the world. I am doing so well and I am happy. I have a beautiful wife.

I feel I am more than 90 per cent better thanks to homeopathy.

CONCLUSION

Homeopathic treatment is often not a single-step event. With homeopathic medicine, good results can occur in a short time provided that the correct remedy is identified and chosen. With modern advancements and innovations in homeopathy, the search for the correct remedy has become much simpler. While improvement might be noticed within a few weeks or months, long-term treatment with an aim to bring very deep results is a process that can take much longer. The aim of homeopathy is not to remove the symptoms alone, but to bring about changes in the entire person. Such changes may not happen from the very first weeks of being prescribed the remedy.

In my experience, the state of the patient generally remains the same until the appropriate homeopathic remedy is given. But when that remedy modifies the state of the patient, we may see another state coming to the surface. So it may not be only a single remedy that cures the patient. At times, the remedy may have to be changed based on the change in the state of the individual. Not every person remains fixed in one state, experience or kingdom his whole life. The kingdoms that we have mentioned do not represent the patient over their whole lifespan. The remedy that is chosen is based on the individual's state at a specific moment in time. For example, a patient could need an animal remedy, but a few months down the line, the symptoms and situations can change into a plant or mineral experience. Similar to the variation in the patient's state and symptoms, the kingdoms are not set in stone and they can change along with the patient as well.

It is not necessary that two homeopaths will come to the same remedy in a given case. This does not mean that one of them is wrong, since more than one remedy can come close enough to the state and experience of the patient to produce an effect. Similar remedies can also work as effectively.

There are many ways of practising homeopathy, and each homeopath chooses the way that is best suited to him. Some follow the traditional homeopathic method with an emphasis on symptoms. Some follow newer ideas such as the classification into kingdoms—plant, mineral and animal. Increasingly, more and more homeopaths are integrating the traditional and contemporary ideas in practice into their own unique eclectic mix.

Sometimes, the homeopath does not get all the

information from the patient the first time. Sometimes, remedy selection may not be accurate or the remedy may work only partially. In these scenarios, during the follow-ups, the homeopath must correctly assess what has or has not happened and observe certain aspects of the case that he may not have noticed before. He has to keep watch for any new phenomena that might come up. The patient might also provide information that he had not given before. It is a cooperative effort, and a process that might involve more than one remedy.

If this book conveys even a slight impression that every case improves dramatically and magically with the first dose given, then I must correct it. This is what we ultimately hope for, but practically we see that it can be a longer process, where the homeopath and the patient work together towards uncovering deeper and deeper aspects, finer and finer symptoms, and then observe what happens after each prescribed remedy is taken.

In chronic or long-standing cases, a six-month period is the outer limit to decide whether a given remedy has had an effect or not. Generally, a homeopath does not remain inactive during this period. He is always alert and watching for more symptoms and experiences, noting the dreams of and the changes in the patient. He also notes down his observations and any information he gets from the patient or the patient's acquaintances. The homeopath is constantly watching if the information he is receiving still pertains to the remedy chosen. If he hears or observes something different, then he re-examines the case, and might change the remedy even before the six-month period. In acute cases, the results are expected within a few days, if not hours, depending on the intensity of the problem. Again, the homeopath remains very alert to any changes and new information, and takes appropriate action.

Therefore, one must not attempt to undertake homeopathic treatment superficially. Also, one must not be dissuaded if the first remedy does not produce dramatic results. By and large, the majority of the patients do very well with homeopathy given sufficient time.

There is one word that is usually missing from a homeopathic interview—the word 'Why'. The homeopath generally does not ask these questions: 'Why do you get angry', 'Why do you have pain in your limbs', 'Why was this disease caused', and so on. The idea of cause and effect does not appeal to the homeopath. He simply studies and observes the phenomenon as it is. It is not why the patient is angry, but what is it that he *experiences* as anger. What is his deepest experience of anger?

By asking the question *what* rather than *why*, we are able to see that each individual has a unique experience of reality; that each one perceives and reacts to external situations in his own unique way. This pattern of perception and reaction is found in every aspect of an individual's life. It does not have a cause. It just *is*. However, it does have a cure. The cure lies in something that is found in nature which reflects this pattern—be it an animal, plant or mineral. When a remedy from that source is administered in ultra-diluted doses, healing takes place.

This is what this book attempts to demonstrate. It is intended to encourage you to look deeply within yourself and perceive the pattern embedded in you, which can be seen in all aspects of your life.

If this book even takes you a few steps in that direction, if you can start seeing how it is not the situation that is the problem but your sensitivity, then you have already taken the first steps towards deep healing.

NOTES

Chapter 1: Traditional Homeopathy

1. Samuel Hahnemann, *Organon of Medicine*, trans. William Boericke (sixth edition, 1921; B. Jain Publishers, 2002), Aphorism 98.

Chapter 3: New Developments in Homeopathy

1. The detailed notes on all the remedies have been sourced from the *Materia Medica*.

Bufo rana is a remedy of the animal kingdom, and is prepared from the toad. These individuals are childish, and if they have any appetite, for food or sexual pleasure, they have to gratify it at once, because they cannot postpone pleasure.

Like other patients needing remedies of the animal kingdom, these individuals have an animated nature, fear of animals and a certain mischievousness. On the one hand, they can be very deceitful, destructive, violent and angry, with a desire to strike. On the other hand, they are foolish and giggly. These individuals have a strong desire for sweets and a characteristic symptom of a crack in the tongue. There is also a tendency towards obesity and convulsions related to the sexual sphere.

2. *Rhus tox* (commonly known as poison ivy) is from the *Anacardiaceae* family. The main sensations of this family include feeling caught, stiffness, tightness, tension, which the opposite sensation of movement ameliorates, and restlessness.

In this remedy, specifically, there is an anticipatory anxiety about something untoward taking place. Individuals belonging to this remedy are superstitious and have many fears: a fear of wrongdoing, being hurt, even being poisoned or murdered. As a result of this anxiety, these individuals cannot sit in one place. They are always moving around, fidgeting—always moving some part of their bodies. There is constant physical restlessness.

From the proving, a key symptom in the patient is feeling worse from initial motion, but better with continued motion. A change of position always makes this patient feel better. Physically, the joints are affected as well as the skin. Being in the poison ivy family, the person experiences intense urticaria and allergic reactions on the skin, which generally get better by heat or hot applications.

Chapter 5: First Impressions

1. *Naja* (prepared from the venom of the Indian cobra) has qualities common to other snake remedies: talkativeness, engaging conversation, malice, jealousy, clairvoyance and the feeling of two wills. Its unique feature is a consciousness of one's duty.

These people have the qualities of nobility, morality and responsibility, but these qualities are in conflict with the feeling of having suffered wrongly and being neglected, with intense feelings of malice and an impulse to neglect or harm the offending person. There is brooding over imaginary troubles and feeling as if they are being neglected or injured.

They also have dreams of snakes and have an interest in or intense fear of snakes. There is clairvoyance and a strong spiritual orientation. *Naja* individuals have a tendency to threaten to strike, but do not do it unless provoked to the extreme. Often *Naja* patients have affections of the heart valves. Physically, they are chilly and cannot tolerate cold air or draughts. (See also chapter 9, n. 1.)

2. *Aurum metallicum* (aka gold) individuals are highly moralistic, principled and orthodox. In these individuals, the feeling is that they must perform tasks that are much beyond their capacity. They are responsible, conscientious, and take their duties very seriously. They can nearly destroy themselves to attain their goal, and if they don't achieve it, they are beset by feelings of failure, guilt and despair. It is as if their very survival depends on their ability to take on these huge responsibilities. These people enjoy music, especially of the religious sort, are neatly turned out, and are perfectionists.

They are punctual in their appointments and the case form is filled out neatly and completely. They get their health check-ups done regularly, and are very meticulous and careful. These patients have a fixed idea about what their duties are, often depending on what they've been taught by their parents. Physically, they develop serious chronic problems such as hypertension, heart disease, and other destructive pathologies.

3. In persons who need *Piper nigrum* as the remedy, there is a feeling of loneliness and boredom and a desire for change, diversion, amusement. The sensation they experience is the one of pain and suffering. Boredom denotes something monotonous, unexciting, bland, tasteless, insipid. They seek amusement and excitement through, parties, pleasure, dancing and other forms of entertainment in order to be cheerful.

4. *Hyoscyamus niger* (commonly known as henbane) is a plant remedy. The main feeling of the patient when proving this remedy is that of being suddenly let down, disappointed, betrayed and deserted by the person on whom he is completely dependent. This situation causes the individual utter fear and panic. It creates a variety of reactions, which are on the one hand winsome, such as loquacity, jesting, seductiveness, etc., and on the other hand threatening, such as a tendency to be violent, or strike, and a desire to kill.

As a result of feeling betrayed, these individuals become highly secretive and protective, aggressive and jealous. There are issues of promiscuity with sexual desire expressed openly, as well as childish and foolish behaviour. These patients are usually jesting, laughing loudly, dancing and inciting others. They are quite suspicious and mistrustful and therefore ask the physician the same question repeatedly.

One of the main aspects of this individual is the feeling of being sexually unattractive. The response to this is uninhibitedly flaunting their sexuality, which they do in an overt, foolish way. The two main proving symptoms of this remedy read as follows: 'One has to disguise himself differently each day, in order to avoid being recognized by those who know him due to the fear of being betrayed.'

Chapter 7: The Problem

1. *Lachesis* is a snake remedy prepared from the venom of the South American bushmaster snake. It has the qualities of aggressiveness, competitiveness, attractiveness, sexuality, deceit, manipulation, and hidden attack, and many other qualities of snakes.

The specific problem of *Lachesis* seems to be the problem of jealousy, or how to get the better of a rival, especially in the sphere of sexual relationships. It is the situation where someone feels the need to compete against a person with better qualities.

These people can be interested in the beauty of nature, in amusement and their speech can be magnetic. A copywriter's mind, for instance, can have the qualities of *Lachesis*, as he is concerned with one-upmanship and jealousy; he amuses, entertains, catches attention, pushing his own product up while cleverly putting other products down, and quickly injects customers with a temptation for the product he's advertising. A large part of the entertainment industry has to do with these themes as well.

The main intention of these individuals is to show off. The ideal situation, which would best give expression to this desire for a *Lachesis* patient would be a beauty contest, where she would try her best to beat out the competition.

Physically, these individuals are often intolerant of heat and may have hot flushes followed by sweating. They cannot tolerate tight clothes (around the neck especially) and they fear being choked or strangled. They are aggravated by exposure to the sunlight and from waking up from sleep. On observation, the tongue protrudes rapidly in and out of the mouth while these individuals speak.

Chapter 9: Dreams and Fears

1. For instance, a prover of the remedy *Naja* had (see chapter 5, n. 1) had the following dream. The prover, a doctor, dreamt that she was staying as a paying guest in the house of an old woman. Around midnight, the latter asked the prover to vacate her room immediately without giving her any reason or explanation. In fact, she started to pick up the prover's belongings and throw them down the stairs, literally pushing her out of the house in the middle of the night. In doing so, the landlady tumbled down the stairs and broke her leg. She started shouting for help. The prover was then caught in a conflict between her duty and responsibility as a doctor, which prompted her to go to the aid of the landlady,

and her impulse to neglect her and make her suffer for the wrong that she had done to her. She woke up from this dream, feeling this 'split' in her mind.

Chapter 12: Childhood

1. Someone needing the remedy *Baryta carbonica* (commonly known as *Barium carbonate*), from the mineral kingdom, is totally dependent on others, almost like an imbecile or someone who's crippled.

The main feeling is that of dependence. There is a feeling of total incapacity to take on responsibilities or do one's own work. They have anticipatory anxiety because of this feeling of incapacity. Individuals needing this medicine are late to take on their responsibilities.

These patients are simple and naive, totally irresolute and depend on someone else to make decisions for them. There is a fear of strangers, fear of facing new situations, and fear of making decisions or choices. They are so dependent, it is childish. These patients like to confirm every single detail during a consultation, for instance, when and how to take the medicine, what are the food restrictions, etc., down to the last detail, often provoking laughter from others.

Often these patients will give a history of being extremely shy in childhood and being unable to mix with others or make friends easily. They feel criticized and have many fears, especially about being laughed at. Physically, they are sensitive to cold with symptoms of premature ageing: hair fall, baldness, loss of memory, hypertension and atherosclerosis at a young age. They desire sweets, yet may be emaciated.

Chapter 13: Lifestyle

1. *Bryonia* is a plant remedy. The main feeling of this individual is one of loss, which has to be made up very fast. The most common way to make up this loss is by doing business. The concentration is entirely on business, so much so that the *Bryonia* person talks and dreams only of doing business.

He is very industrious, busy and determined to make the most money and build his enterprise. He works at a feverish pace and becomes dry and insensitive to the emotions and feelings of others. He talks very little and does not like to be disturbed. He reads things concerned with this topic alone, converses mostly with business-oriented people, and his attitude in the clinic too is businesslike.

These individuals take risks. There is a fear of poverty, and feelings of avarice towards those who have more than them. They dream of being busy, of exertion both mental and physical, and of constantly doing business. The physical complaints of these individuals are acute and will impede movement. These individuals desire warm milk and soups.

2. *Plumbum metallicum* (commonly known as lead) is a remedy from the mineral kingdom. It is one of the heaviest minerals in the Periodic Table of the Elements. This individual has the feeling that he is no ordinary person—he is a king or a ruler of the highest order.

There is a theme of attack and defence, but in such an extreme degree that the person feels that everyone is conspiring against him. He feels that murderers surround him, and that everyone is conspiring to murder him. This creates in him an intense state of anxiety and he gets extremely fearful dreams.

This may be the actual situation of a person who has absolute power, like the head of a country who is ultimately assassinated. The *Plumbum* person feels attacked and has to defend himself against the same. There are symptoms of striking others and violent behaviour. They are also great performers, leaders and kings.

On the physical plane, pathology manifests as paralysis which is slowly occurring, as well as degeneration of the nerves. There is destruction with loss of power in the limbs. In fact, lead poisoning is shown to produce paralysis. They also have constipation and a characteristic blue line on the gums, called the 'lead line'. These individuals often desire to eat fried things.

Chapter 15: Analysis

1. Robert W. Matthews and Janice R. Matthews, *Insect Behavior* (New York: Springer, 2010; 2nd edn).

FURTHER READING

Allen, H.C. *Materia Medica of Nosodes*. Delhi: B. Jain Publishers, 2004.

Boericke, W. *Pocket Manual of Homoeopathic Materia Medica*. Delhi: B. Jain Publishers, 2009.

Boger, C.M. *A Synoptic Key to the Materia Medica*. Delhi: B. Jain Publishers, 2002.

Kent, J.T. *Repertory of the Homeopathic Materia Medica*. Delhi: Educa Books/B. Jain Publishers, 2003.

Phatak, S.R. *A Concise Repertory of Homoeopathic Medicines*. Delhi: B. Jain Publishers, 2002.

———. *Materia Medica of Homoeopathic Medicines*. Delhi: B. Jain Publishers, 1988.

Sankaran, R. *An Insight into Plants*. Vols 1–3. Mumbai: Homoeopathic Medical Publishers, 2005.

———. *From Similia to Synergy*. Mumbai: Homoeopathic Medical Publishers, 2013.

————. *Homoeopathy for Today's World: Discovering Your Animal, Mineral, or Plant Nature*. Mumbai: Healing Arts Press, Homoeopathic Medical Publishers, 2011.

————. *Homoeopathy: The Science of Healing*. Delhi: B. Jain Publishers, 2005.

————. *Structure: Experiences with the Mineral Kingdom*. Vols 1 and 2. Mumbai: Homoeopathic Medical Publishers, 2008.

————. *The Other Song: Discovering Your Parallel Self*. Mumbai: Homoeopathic Medical Publishers, 2009.

————. *The Sensation in Homoeopathy*. Mumbai: Homoeopathic Medical Publishers, 2004.

————. *The Soul of Remedies*. Mumbai: Homoeopathic Medical Publishers, 1997.

————. *The Spirit of Homoeopathy*. Mumbai: Homoeopathic Medical Publishers, 1999.

————. *The Substance of Homoeopathy*. Mumbai: Homoeopathic Medical Publishers, 1994.

————. *The Synergy in Homeopathy*. Mumbai: Homoeopathic Medical Publishers, 2012.

Sankaran, R., and M. Shah. *Survival: The Reptile*. Vols 1 and 2. Mumbai: Homoeopathic Medical Publishers, 2011.